Colonial Yorktown

1881
The Victory Monument,
Yorktown, Va.

Colonial Yorktown

CLYDE F. TRUDELL

Illustrated by the Author

THE CHATHAM PRESS, INC.

Old Greenwich, Connecticut

DISTRIBUTED BY THE VIKING PRESS, INC., NEW YORK

SBN 85699-019-1 Hardbound Edition
SBN 85699-020-5 Paperbound Edition

Library of Congress Catalog Card Number 75-135964

Colonial Yorktown is produced in cooperation with
The United States Department of the Interior,
National Park Service and the Colonial National
Historical Park.

Manufactured in the United States of America

Contents

PREFACE . . .   7

INTRODUCTION . . .   9

THE YORK RIVER . . . 13

RINGFIELD . . . 17

BELLFIELD . . . 21

KISKIACK . . . 28

YORKTOWN . . . 37

GRACE EPISCOPAL CHURCH . . . 57

THE THOMAS SESSIONS HOUSE . . . 63

THE ARCHER COTTAGE . . . 70

THE THOMAS PATE HOUSE . . . 73

THE CUSTOM HOUSE . . . 76

THE DUDLEY DIGGES HOUSE . . . 84

THE MUNGO SOMERWELL HOUSE . . . 89

THE SWAN TAVERN . . . 95

THE NELSON HOUSE . . . 106

THE EDMUND SMITH HOUSE . . . 111

THE CAPTAIN JOHN BALLARD HOUSE . . . 115

THE COURTHOUSE . . . 118

THE MEDICAL SHOP . . . 124

WINDMILL POINT . . . 128

THE SIEGE OF 1781 . . . 131

THE MOORE HOUSE . . . 142

THE VICTORY MONUMENT . . . 151

THE PENINSULAR CAMPAIGN OF 1862 . . . 156

THE NAVAL WEAPONS STATION . . . 167

THE SESQUICENTENNIAL OF 1931 . . . 171

THE JAMESTOWN-WILLIAMSBURG-YORKTOWN
CELEBRATION OF 1957 . . . 175

COLONIAL NATIONAL HISTORICAL PARK: 1970 . . . 179

APPENDIX . . . 181

The Significance of Yorktown
Articles of Capitulation (1781)
Original Purchasers of Lots
Bibliography

INDEX . . . 189

Dedicated to Martha, my wife.

Preface

S INCE the first publication of *Colonial Yorktown* in 1938, considerable documentary research has made available additional information of historical significance that corrects and augments the material incorporated in the book at that earlier date. The subsequent development of Colonial National Historical Park, the 350th Anniversary Celebration of Jamestown in 1957, and the build up of reference material in the Park Library all have demonstrated the desirability of a revised and more authentic record of Yorktown.

In the preparation of this revised edition the author has had at his disposal the facilities of Colonial National Historical Park and readily acknowledges his indebtedness to the Park Staff for their courtesy and cooperation. He feels particularly obligated to Charles E. Hatch, Jr., National Park Service Historian, and Dr. Edward M. Riley of Colonial Williamsburg for the privilege of being allowed to refer to their comprehensive and definitive material on the old buildings of Yorktown; to James N. Haskett, Chief Park Historian, for his friendly and helpful suggestions in preparing the revisions; and to Mrs. Bernice Ketner for her assistance in using the Park files.

While every effort has been made toward historical accuracy, the author must regretfully claim any errors as his own.

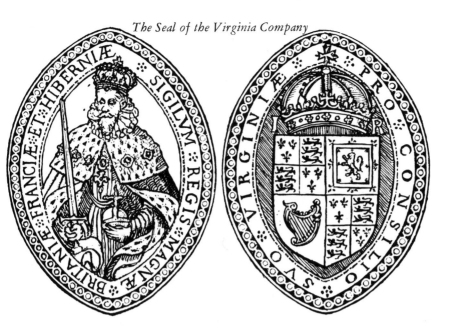

The Seal of the Virginia Company

Introduction

T HE history of Yorktown is Virginia's history in miniature. It is the story of exploration and discovery; of Indian fights and hardships among the first settlers; of tobacco and the great plantations. It is the tale of her two neighbors, Jamestown and Williamsburg, and the recording of a growing spirit of independence. Finally, it is the story of the Revolution.

There have been so many years of war in the life of Yorktown that, in the popular mind, the little village must always be associated with the color and pageantry of military history. But there were also the long years of peace, now almost forgotten, when the town was equally as colorful in the pageantry that attended its station as a thriving tobacco port of the eighteenth century.

Among the names of Yorktown's early citizens, sometimes representing an individual, sometimes an entire family, and oftentimes families whose members were distinguished in generation after generation, we find the Nelsons, the Reads, Nicolas Martiau, Philip Lightfoot, the Wests, the Smiths, the Ludlows, the Digges and a host of others, each of whom wrote a full page in the history of Virginia.

Yorktown has been censured for her habit of living in the past,

9

for basking in the reflected glories of a more glamorous age. For her it is not the past but a manner of thought and living that has proven adequate; the customs and thoughts of yesteryear are not dead mannerisms but lively issues of the present.

Our statesmen in Washington boil and stew this very day over opposing interpretations of the Constitution. To Yorktown it is merely a continuance of the controversy that began in 1788 with a three-week battle of words in the Convention assembled at Richmond to ratify the Constitution.

Do we hear cries of attempted dictatorship in the political arena? They are but echoes to Yorktown of the selfsame cries that sounded throughout Tidewater when some claimed Patrick Henry intended to set up a dictatorship and Archibald Cary, "Old Iron of Ampthill," threatened that the day of Henry's appointment as dictator "shall be the day of his death, for he shall find my dagger in his heart before the sunset of that day."

Our current problems in agriculture are old stories to Yorktown. She remembers when crop control was practiced in the tobacco culture of Colonial days to raise prices and suit the supply to the demand.

The very bell that tolled York burghers to worship, almost a hundred years before Cornwallis and his army despoiled the town, still peals forth from the belfry of old Grace Episcopal Church and the "dugout" fishing boats of the York are but replicas of their eighteenth century prototypes.

The use of Yorktown and the York River as a harbor for our fleets during all of our wars impressed the good folk of York not at all. For a river that had already witnessed the wide sails of the Spanish conquistadores, the first English ships bearing Captains Newport and John Smith, the pirate fleet of Blackbeard, the palatial barges of the tobacco planters, the transports of Earl Cornwallis and the troop ships of McClellan, another fleet, however modern, was but so many more ships in the endless armada that has sailed the York River and the Chesapeake waterways.

Massachusetts may flaunt her Concord, her Lexington, and Bunker Hill; Pennsylvania her Brandywine and Valley Forge; and New York her Saratoga and Ticonderoga. Virginia smugly has the last word with the surrender of Cornwallis at Yorktown.

10

The confirmed cosmopolite, staunch in his belief that nothing lasts, nothing is permanent, will cut a new facet to his philosophy by lingering for a spell along the shores of the York. Beyond the mad whirlpool of modern existence Yorktown remains a quiet eddy, little affected by the great commotion.

Our memory sees more than our eye in this place where so much that was now is gone. Few of the old houses remain but those few are protected and cared for with almost a religious devotion. There has been an awakening to the value and importance of Virginia's historic landmarks and a movement is afoot to save what is left before it is too late.

Paul Wilstach has posed this current picture so effectively in his *Tidewater Virginia* that we take the liberty to quote from his book:

> . . . this renaissance is the budding of an idea. The idea is the salvage of something precious, the salvage of something verging on disappearance. And that something is precious, moreover, because it is not only local but national, and belongs to every American.

The idea extends to Yorktown, but while preserving and restoring a few of the colonial buildings, the town will not be changed. It will remain apart from the modern scene, a haven from the hurry and worry of life "where the past emerges from its centuries and puts on the mantle of reality."

For those who make the pilgrimage to Yorktown, and for those who find pleasurable reading in the recorded word of bygone events, this book is intended.

1524
Verrazano,
in the river
now called the
York.

The York River

"**F**OURTEENE miles Northward from the river Powhatan is the river Pamaunke which is navigable 60 or 70 myles, but with Catches and small Barkes 30 or 40 myles farther . . . on the south side of this river is Chiskiack . . ." So wrote John Smith in recording his explorations of 1607, giving us the earliest specific reference to the York River and Yorktown, for the "Pamaunke" became first the Charles and then the York River, and the "Chiskiack" area which included the present site of Yorktown, while the "river Powhatan" has become the mighty James.

Long before John Smith penetrated the peaceful waters of the York, the river had been visited by other white men who, after a hazardous crossing of the Atlantic, entered Chesapeake Bay just as Smith and Newport had when blown by a storm to the Virginia shore in 1607.

Under commission from King Henry VII, John Cabot sailed out of Bristol in 1498 and reached land on this side of the ocean. Cruising south along the coast he made record of a "great bay" that, in all probability, was the Chesapeake. After having come all that way it is reason-

13

able to presume that he looked around a bit and made at least sketchy forays into the waterways that led off from that great bay seeking, as did every early voyager to these shores, the "Northwest Passage."

At about the same time Amerigo Vespucci had reached the coast of Florida and, muttering in his beard over this unexpected landfall, sailed up the long unbroken coast seeking an inward avenue for his ships to continue westward. His northernmost reach has long been identified with the waters of the Chesapeake.

Twenty-six years later another Italian, Verrazano, is believed to have explored these shores to be closely followed within two years by the Spaniard, Ayallon, who entered a great harbor and, after exploring its numerous waterways, attempted a settlement which he called San Miguel de Gualdape; and there are those who claim that San Miguel was on the identical site where years later Jamestown was founded.

After Menendez de Aviles had established St. Augustine in Florida in the year 1566, he sent an expedition up the coast to what he called "St. Mary Bay," the waters of which were unmistakably the Chesapeake because seven years later they were described in detail by another Spaniard, Barcia, who explored the coast in 1573 and located St. Mary Bay as being thirty-seven and one-half degrees north and "it is three leagues wide and you enter it N.N.W.; within there are many rivers and harbors on both sides where a vessel can enter." This description is as apt today as it was when written about four hundred years ago.

In September, 1570, a party of nine Spanish Jesuits are said to have entered the James River and landed at College Creek. They then crossed the peninsula to establish a mission on the York River. Six months later all were massacred by the Indians, save one young boy who was eventually rescued by the Spanish.

John Smith was not the first Englishman to visit the Chesapeake country because Captain Lane of Raleigh's Croatan Colony in Carolina came as far north as the bay in 1585 and viewed "the country of the Chesepiooks."

Although others had preceded him as visitors, Smith had the distinction of being the first to explore thoroughly and record descriptively the waterways of the Chesapeake.

The York is the shortest of the main rivers that lead into Chesapeake Bay, coursing through that section of Virginia most glamorous in romance and history, the Tidewater — a low country where tidal waters wind through a gently undulating land to the sea, forming all that territory contiguous to Chesapeake Bay; a section one hundred and sixty miles long and one hundred and twenty wide, where fact and fancy have become so interwoven it is well nigh impossible to tell for certain where the one ends and the other begins.

The James, Rappahannock, and Potomac serve the cities of Richmond, Fredericksburg, and Washington. All three rivers know modern river traffic and the commercial scenes of the present. The York retains much of its original appearance; and there are many stretches that still preserve the peaceful wooded shore devoid of habitation or any sign of man's intrusion, much as John Smith first viewed it from the little pinnace that carried him into all of the quiet waters leading out from Chesapeake Bay.

Dignified by name as a river, the York is actually little more than an elongated estuary of the Bay, having no current but the ebb and flow of the tide. Except at its head, where it is fed by the Pamunkey and Mataponi rivers, the York is salty and brackish; and should its fresh water sources cease to flow, the York would remain because its real source is the ocean. In fact, as Chesapeake Bay is only an irregularity of the coast that allows the Atlantic to penetrate inland and the York is a branch of the Bay, it might in truth be said that the York River is but a part of the Atlantic Ocean. By anchoring a ship in Hampton Roads at the mouth of the river during the ebb period and hoisting anchor with the incoming of the tide, it is possible to navigate the entire length of the York without employing any other power than the tidal flow.

The river is lined now, as it was in Smith's day, along both shores by heavily wooded areas of beech, oak, cedar, maple, walnut, the inevitable pine, and a profusion of shrubs, vines, berries, and many kinds of colorful wild flowers.

Having one of the deepest natural channels in the world, the York has offered anchorage to a long succession of historic fleets. The merchant ships forming the great tobacco fleets of the early Virginia Colony left the safety of the York to be convoyed by men-of-war beyond the Capes and the threat of pirate attack; during the uprising of 1676, Sir William Berkeley sought refuge on his vessels in the York, and the

15

Earl Lord Cornwallis trusted the York to provide safe anchorage for his transports in his investment of Yorktown in 1781. Comte de Grasse took advantage of that same quality of the river by blockading the Bay, keeping Cornwallis penned up in the river. In the War of 1812, the British Fleet again assailed the waters of the Chesapeake and from the York might have been witnessed the passage of the English ships bound for the burning of Washington. During the Civil War the York was the base of operations for McClellan in his abortive Peninsular Campaign; and Hampton Roads, at the mouth of the river, provided the scene of a naval battle that will be recalled as long as naval history is written; for here, in Hampton Roads, the *Monitor* and the *Merrimac* demonstrated that a new era, the age of metal ships, was at hand. The United States Navy made the York a base of supplies for its immense transport service during World War I and from it conducted the operations attending the barrage of the North Sea. Today it is the locale of the U.S. Naval Weapons Station.

To this river then, in 1607, came Captain John Smith, he of the photographic eye and the curiosity of the magpie. "On the south side of this river is Chiskiack," he wrote, and it is to the south side of the river and the fortunes of the Chiskiack area that we devote our attention in this "brief historie."

There is a method of writing history, attributed by Van Loon to the French, that favors compilation. "Let us compile," they say, "and out of seven hundred and forty-two books make a seven hundred and forty-third." It is almost impossible to attempt telling this story without adopting some method similar to the compilation of the French because nowhere does the complete story exist between two covers. While this volume cannot begin to claim any pretensions towards completeness, it has been prepared with every care for authentic sources and will serve its purpose in stimulating a more competent narrator to prepare the comprehensive type of work on Yorktown that its history and people so heartily deserve.

1660
Ringfield,
near Yorktown, Virginia.

Ringfield

A T a very early date there had been a tendency among the colonists toward outward expansion away from Jamestown and a general movement to establish plantations and places of residence throughout Tidewater. One of the first adventurers to establish himself upon the south shore of the York River was a well-known sea captain from London named Robert Felgate who obtained patent in 1630 to the land lying between the fork of King's Creek and the creek that now bears his own name, some six miles west or up the river from the present site of Yorktown.

Most of this land is composed of salt marshes, mud flats, and swamp; but about one hundred acres of elevated solid ground borders the river and provides an ideal house site, commanding magnificent views of the water and benefiting by cool winds in summer.

After Captain Felgate's death in 1644 the estate was disposed of and eventually, around 1655, became the property of his nephew, William Felgate. After William's death, his widow married Captain John Underhill whose property the estate became. Underhill lies buried on the land and until recent years his tombstone was visible. The land was

17

acquired in 1693 by Joseph Ring, and it was from Ring that the plantation took the name of Ringfield, by which it is still known.

Joseph Ring was a man of prominence in the early affairs of York County. A year before he had acquired the old Felgate property the King's Council had appointed him, together with Lieutenant Colonel Thomas Ballard, as a Trustee of the newly formed port of Yorktown. The duty of the two Trustees was to sell, for one hundred and eighty pounds each, the eighty-five lots of the town that had been surveyed and laid off by Major Lawrence Smith and to see that the covenant requiring building during the first year was kept.

These services were rendered with such commendable zeal and efficiency that the Council gave both Ring and Ballard a town lot each in recognition of their good work. Joseph Ring was given Lot No. 10 but whether or not he built a town house on it is not known.

Back on his acres at Ringfield, or Ring's Neck as it was sometimes called, he did build a very fine house. It was a brick structure two and a half stories high that was approached between a long avenue of cedars. This house, first mentioned in his will of December 3, 1698, stood for over two hundred years until it was destroyed by fire in the 1920's.

Ringfield adjoined the famous E. D. Plantation of Governor Edward Digges. Joseph Ring was such a good friend to his exalted neighbor that when Digges died the Court selected Ring as one of the three men appointed to divide the Digges estate at Bellfield among the widow and children.

The Ring manor house occupied an unusually fine site with a panoramic view of the river. From the house the land sloped gently down to reedy marshes that even today make ideal retreats for water fowl. In Ring's day, during the migrating season, the skies were darkened for hours at a time by the millions of ducks and geese in their southward flight.

Nothing now remains of the famous old house but the foundations. The sketch heading this chapter is based upon a picture that was taken before the building was destroyed by fire and appears in Lancaster's *Historic Virginia Homes and Churches*.

A short distance from the house site are the remains of the tombstone of Joseph Ring who died February 26, 1703, and the tombstones of his two sons, Edmund and Isack.

Exploratory investigation about the house site has discovered fragments of paneling, window sash and shutters, a paneled door and wrought iron "H" hinges with ornamented terminations; all of which suggest that the original manse was in its time a house of elegance and dignity.

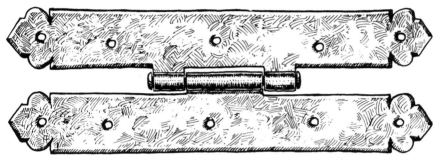

Ornamental wrought-iron hinge from Ringfield.

Ringfield, Bellfield, Kiskiack, the plantation of Read, and those around old Yorke at Wormley Creek were the scattered groups of settlements that made necessary the selecting of a common port and formation of an organized community, leading finally to the creation of Yorktown in 1691.

The grave of Nathaniel Bacon, Sr., is supposed to be near Ringfield, and at one time his tombstone was taken from the grave and kept on view near the house. It has since been removed to the tower of Bruton Parish Church in Williamsburg. A commemorative marker was placed in the Ringfield burial ground for Nathaniel Bacon, Sr. and Joseph Ring in 1946 by the state of Virginia. The estate passed through various and sundry ownerships until 1820 when it came into the possession of that inveterate realtor and Baptist preacher, Scervant Jones, who mortgaged the property to William Waller.

19

There is no record of the lands subsequently being released or conveyed from the Jones ownership; but it is known that prior to the War Between the States the property belonged to Thomas Garland Tinsley, under whose ownership the estate became known as Lansdowne. To satisfy the terms of Tinsley's will which provided that his estate be divided between his children, Thomas, Alexander, Seaton, and Harriet, the entire property was surveyed and divided into a number of tracts in 1867. The division marked "B" contained the 117½ acres that included the old Ringfield house.

Since the above mentioned division the Ringfield portion passed through seventeen different ownerships until April 30, 1920, when it was conveyed to the United States Government as a part of the Navy Mine Depot. It is now the Naval Weapons Station, administered under special permit from the U.S. Navy by the National Park Service. The division marked "A", containing some 120 acres, was the old colonial church parish glebe land that had been added to the estate prior to 1820 and now serves as Park picnic grounds.

Bellfield, near Yorktown, Virginia.

Bellfield

IN the early days of the Colony, when Captain John Smith was having his maps of Virginia engraved with "Pamaunk flu" to designate the river that was to become known as the Charles and finally the York, members of the Pamunkey tribe, for whom the river was first named, lived along its banks.

Encouraged by the government at Jamestown and the Court Order of 1630, Captain John West, one of the three West brothers, obtained patent to that part of Kiskiack later to be called Bellfield, bordering Felgate's Creek a few miles up river from what was to become, sixty years later, the site of Yorktown. After Captain Robert Felgate, John West became the second settler in 1630 to take up 600 acres of land at Chiskiack on the Pamunkey River in the very heart of the hostile Indian country.

Captain John West was brother to Lord De la Warre, the personage we recognize in our history books as Lord Delaware, who was commissioned on February 28, 1610, to succeed Sir Thomas Gates as Governor of the Virginia Colony, administering the Crown's interests from Jamestown.

A third, younger, West brother was the "Capteyne Francis West" whom John Smith had sent in 1609 "with one hundrethe and fortye men upp to the falls with sixe monthes victewells to inhabitt there." This reference was to the falls of the James River at the approximate present site of the City of Richmond.

A fort was built, but after its building Francis West quarreled with the Honorable George Percy, and it was necessary for Captain John Smith to come up from Jamestown to settle the dispute. Rather than yield to his subordinate, Smith abandoned the entire project and thus ended the first attempted settlement at the "falles."

The King's Council granted Captain John West two thousand acres in 1632 "in right of his son being the first born Christian at Chischiack." John West's son, Lieutenant Colonel John West, was the first child born of English parents on the York River.

From the time of his arrival in 1618 at the colony aboard the *Bonny Bess*, Captain West was associated with the military and, after the Indian massacre of 1622, commanded a company of men in the reprisals against the savages. He was a member of the House of Burgesses, 1629-30; member of the Council, 1631; Justice of York County, 1634; and after the colonists had thrust out Governor Sir John Harvey, West served as Governor in 1635-36.

Captain John West and his wife, Anne, sold their broad plantation of 1,250 acres to Edward Digges on September 11, 1650, and moved to their second plantation at the fork of the York River on the site of the present town of West Point, where the Captain died in 1659.

Their son, Lieutenant Colonel John West, was loyal to Governor Berkeley during Bacon's Rebellion and sat as a member of the courts-martial which tried the insurgents. He served New Kent County in the House of Burgesses in 1685. In 1667 he married Unity Croshaw, daughter of Major Joseph Croshaw of York County, and died in 1691 at the West Point Plantation.

Edward Digges was the son of Sir Dudley Digges of Chilham in England. Sir Dudley was Master of the Rolls to King Charles I and a member of the London Company. In 1632 King Charles had appointed Sir Dudley to a Council of Superintendence over Virginia empowered to ascertain the condition of the Colony. So his son, Edward, came to Virginia not entirely ignorant of conditions to be coped with in the wilderness.

Five years after Edward Digges bought the West Plantation he was made Governor of the Virginia Colony, becoming the second of the three governors to hold that office under the regime of Cromwell. Edward Digges succeeded Bennet to the governorship, the latter having been appointed an agent of the Colony in London. During his term of office Digges received a salary of twenty-five thousand pounds of tobacco together with certain duties levied from masters of vessels, called "castle duties," and marriage license fees.

After his term of governor, Digges also was sent to England in 1657 as the agent of the Colony, carrying with him the high esteem of the colonists. Through his many virtues he enjoyed the confidence, respect, and affection of the people who testified in a letter to Oliver Cromwell, the Lord Protector, that Digges had managed his government in Virginia with "Much moderation, prudence and justice."

While in England Digges influenced the merchants there to pay a higher price for tobacco of superior quality rather than a standard price regardless of quality as was the custom. This encouraged the Virginia planters to increase the quality rather than the quantity of their crops.

Digges was one of the more enlightened plantation owners who foresaw the complete exhaustion of the soil by continual tobacco growing. Experimenting with various tobacco cultures, he was credited with producing the best tobacco shipped to England. His estate produced the famous "E. D." (Edward Digges) tobacco which "never failed to bring in England one shilling when other tobacco would not bring three pence." The Digges plantation was always known as the "E. D. Plantation" until it was sold by William Digges, Jr., in 1787, and in the title deed of that sale it is first denominated as Bellfield, the name it has carried to this day.

The authority of the Governor's office, which he held for the two years 1655 and 1656, gave Edward Digges an opportunity to further the establishment of a silk industry in Virginia. To this end he imported Armenians skilled in the silk culture and supported an Act requiring that, for every hundred acres held in fee simple, ten mulberry trees should be planted by every plantation owner. Thousands of mulberry trees were consequently imported and planted, silk worms introduced from abroad, and a bounty of "five thousand pounds of tobacco out of the public levie" was offered to "what person soever should first make one hundred pounds of wound silk in one yeare within this Colony." Interest had been alive to the possibilities of the silk culture, and the Colony had already "received good store of silkeworme seed both out of Fraunce, Italy and Spaine," and "eight French Vignerons from Languedock who are very skillful also in breeding silke-wormes and making silke." In 1622 one of these Frenchmen, John Bonoeil, prepared a "Treatise of the Art of making Silke, OR, Directions for the making of lodgings, and the breeding, nourishing, and ordering of Silkewormes, and for the planting of Mulberry trees, and all other things belonging to the Silke Art."

But Edward's industry failed. Either the silk worms did not like his mulberry trees or the trees did not think well of Virginia. At any rate the worms toiled not neither did they spin, and the trees fell into a heavy melancholy that proved fatal to the greater number of them. Legend records some success because the coronation robes of Charles II were purported to have been partly made of Virginia silk. The infant industry languished and was short lived, but the survivors among the mulberry trees remain scattered throughout all Tidewater and in their gnarled and scraggly fashion mutely testify to the energy with which one man endeavored to make an actuality of his dreams.

Governor Digges later served as Auditor General for the Colony and was a member of the King's Council until his death. He departed this life in 1675 and lies buried under one of the four massive tombs at Bellfield in the Digges family burial ground. These tombstones and the foundations of his manor house are all that remain to mark the site of one of the most extensive and widely known plantations of seventeenth century Tidewater Virginia. Gone the proud manse! Vanished the cultivated acres on acres of growing tobacco. *Sic transit gloria mundi!*

The four Digges tombs at Bellfield mark the last resting places of Governor Edward; Dudley, his second son; Susanne, the wife of Dudley; and Cole Digges, deceased 1744.

Joseph Ring of Ringfield, the plantation on the York nearest to Bellfield, was appointed by the Court to assist in the division of the estate of Governor Edward Digges' widow. She had survived her illustrious husband and all but three of their thirteen children. At her death her son-in-law, Captain Francis Page, petitioned the Court for a division of the estate in behalf of his daughter, Elizabeth. The division was accordingly made, and an inventory entered in the York County records at the time, August 24, 1692, listed a fortune of £1102/18/10 together with the manor house and plantation, 108 slaves, and all of the furnishings of the manor house with its "hall parlor, ye low passage, yellow roome, large roome against ye yellow roome, ye back rooms against ye large roome, the red roome, the garretts, the back roome, the sellar and the kitching."

The epitaph of Governor Digges, written by his wife, reads:

> To the memory of Edward Digges, Esquire, Sonne of Sir Dudley Digges of Chilham in Kent, Knight and Baronet, Master of the Rolle in the reign of King Charles the 1st. He departed this life the 15th day of March, 1676 in the 55th year of his age, one of his Majesty's Council for this his Colony of Virginia. A Gentleman of most commendable parts and ingenuity and the only introducer and promoter of the silk-manufacture in this colonie, and in everything else a pattern worthy of all pious imitation. He had six sonnes and seven daughters by the body of his wife, Elizabeth, who of her conjugal affection hath dedicated to him this memorial.

The plantation remained in the Digges family and preserved its ancient limits for more than one hundred years, but after the Revolution the family fortunes declined; the estate was finally sold under the name of Bellfield in 1787 by William Digges, Jr., to William Waller.

In 1811, the land was owned and advertised for sale by the Baptist preacher, the Reverend Scervant Jones, who a few years later also bought the neighboring plantation of Ringfield.

Although little now remains of the original estate of the Digges' at Bellfield, it must have been pretentious and elaborate, indeed, in the Governor's time. The manor house burned in the middle of the eighteenth century; the ruins were razed to the ground, and a second structure was erected on a different but nearby site.

In 1918 the land was purchased by the United States Government and it became a part of the Navy Mine Depot, now the Naval Weapons Station.

When the Navy took over Bellfield, the eighteenth century structure was still standing, and being of frame construction, it was considered a potential fire hazard and was razed. The sketch heading this chapter was made from a photograph of this later building taken before the house was demolished by the Navy.

Archaelogical excavations conducted by the National Park Service in connection with their work at Yorktown disclosed and uncovered for study the foundations of both the seventeenth and eighteenth century structures, and the most casual observation of the extent and thickness of the massive brick foundations of the earlier structure is convincing proof that Edward Digges lived indeed like a "royal" governor at "E. D. Plantation."

The foundations of the seventeenth century house measure thirty-four feet in width and forty-seven feet in length with brick foundation walls twenty-eight inches thick laid up in Flemish bond and glazed headers. The entire basement was brick paved, and from the several types of molded brick and square brick hearth tiles found among the excavations we can imagine the elegance of the superstructure.

Governor Digges' eldest son, William, Captain of Horse in 1676 during Bacon's Rebellion, was a soldier of no mean ability and during the Rebellion fought a hand-to-hand engagement with Thomas Hansford, one of Bacon's lieutenants, cutting off one of his adversary's fingers in the fight. William Digges later served as Sheriff of York County in 1679 and finally settled in Maryland.

Bellfield was used during World War I as an Aviation Training Camp and was then considered by naval fliers as one of the best landing fields in the country.

On this tract of land at Bellfield has been enacted every stage and period of growth in the settlement, development, flourishing, and final decline of the typical Colonial Virginia tobacco plantation. Starting with its original occupation as part of the Indian lands of Kiskiack, it developed from a pioneer's settlement under the Wests to a prosperous tobacco plantation under Edward Digges. With the Revolution it declined to the status of a typical slave-holding estate of *ante-bellum* days. Then came the Civil War and the gradual abandonment of agricultural activity until now the proud lands of Bellfield have gone completely back to forest.

Giant Silver Poplar,
Bellfield near Yorktown,
Virginia.

1641
Kiskiack,
near Yorktown
Virginia.

The first Lee Home in America.

Kiskiack

ON John Smith's first map of Virginia the locale around Yorktown is noted "Kiskiack," although in his writings he referred to this section as Chiskiack. Other writers have used such spellings as Chesiak, Chischiacke, Kiskyache, Kiskiak, Kis-Kiskiak, and even the corruption of corruptions, Cheese-cake. With philologists still quarreling among themselves over the proper meaning of the word "Chesapeake" we hesitate to advance a definite interpretation of "Kiskiack." Having little knowledge of Indian terminal generics, we are content to accept the generally adopted meaning "broad or flat land" which, indeed, describes the land above Yorktown. The name applied not so much to a definite site on the river as to all the territory inhabited by the Kiskiack Indians. They lent their name to the tribal chieftain or "werowance," whom Smith called "Chescaik" although this apellation was also subject to various spellings.

Often hostile to the first settlers, the Kiskiacks discouraged any attempts at permanent settlement along the York. To thwart this menacing attitude of the Indians, the taking up of land along the York was stimulated by a Court Order of October 8, 1630, which offered fifty acres to every colonist who would take up residence for a year in

28

"the Forest . . . for securing and taking in a tract of land, bounding upon the Chiefe residence of the Pamunkey King, the most dangerous head of the Indian enemye" and twenty-five additional acres if the colonist was still alive the second year.

With the doughty Captain Felgate, a London skipper, taking the initiative and supported by John Utie, the West brothers, Henry Lee, and Nicholas Martiau, land was gradually taken up and patented along the York, and the Indians were slowly but surely driven from that section to the opposite side of the river.

Ottahotin,
Chief of the Pamunkeys, the
Chickahominies and Kiskiacks

The first settlement along the York retained the original Indian name of Kiskiack. To this wilderness came Henry Lee, obtaining patent in 1641 to two hundred and fifty acres of land to which he was entitled because, pursuant of the Court Order of 1630, he had brought five persons to settle with him. He cleared lands and built the snug little brick house that still stands, the oldest Lee house in America. It is one of the best small examples of mid-seventeenth century brick architecture in Tidewater. The story and a half structure has dormer windows, interesting chimneys at either gable, and fine brick-work.

Nine generations of Lees have called the old house at Kiskiack their home, and it is impossible to visit the site without experiencing profound stirrings of the imagination. In a section where it took only twenty-five years from "farm to forest," this old plantation has remained long untended; and the forest has closed in all around the house, giving the location very much the appearance it must have had before the land was cleared and Henry Lee dared move into the heart of the Indian country.

There is no documentary evidence of any family connection between Henry Lee of Kiskiack and Richard Lee of Northumberland, although both were originally from Shropshire, England. Richard was to become the common ancestor of the two Lees who signed the Declaration of Independence, Richard Henry and Francis Lightfoot, and also of Colonel "Light Horse" Harry Lee and his son, General Robert E. Lee.

The Lee House at Kiskiack burned in 1915 completely gutting the interior, but the brick walls remain in an excellent state of preservation. The structure is now within the confines of the Naval Weapons Station. The old Indian tribe is remembered by a broad meadow that still bears the name "Indian Field"; and the Lee house is as often referred to as "old Kiskiack," the last reminder in this section of an almost vanished race.

North of Queen's Creek along the York River above Kiskiack were three early plantations, Ripon Hall, Vaulx Hall, and Porto Bello, all of which now lie within the confines of Camp Peary, the U.S. Naval Construction Training Center for the Seabees of World War II.

The first patentee of this land was one William Prior. He settled just below Carter's Creek (then called St. Andrew's Creek) in 1637 on 600 acres of land that he had been granted by the Crown for transporting a total of twelve persons to the new colony from England in conformance with the Court Order of 1630. The following year title was changed to Major Joseph Croshaw, a son of Captain Raleigh Croshaw, one of the colonists to Jamestown. Croshaw called his holding "Poplar Springs" and, at his death, left the estate to his son-in-law, Colonel John West, a nephew of Lord Delaware. In 1667, under the name "Poplar Neck," the property was sold by West to Edmund Jenings who built thereon a brick house and called it "Ripon Hall" after his ancestral home in Yorkshire, England.

The fortunes of Edmund Jenings of Ripon Hall fill a full page in the annals of Virginia history. He became Attorney General, Member, Secretary and then President of the Council, twice acting Governor of the Colony and member of various committees that revised the laws, treated with the Indians, and represented the colonists in their affairs with the Lords Commissioners of Trade and Plantations, both in Virginia and England. He remained a member of the Council until his death in 1727 at Ripon Hall. He also served as Collector of the Customs and Naval Officer and Receiver of Duties, during which office he originated the great tobacco fleets which sailed in convoys strong enough to resist the attacks of pirates who were numerous at this date.

Edmund Jenings was instrumental in laying out the town of Williamsburg and establishing the College of William and Mary, furnishing the Capitol and many other civic services. He assisted in the building of the first church of Middleton Parish at Middle Plantation, which later became Williamsburg, was vestryman and held a family pew. By his marriage he established one of the First Families of Virginia and was the direct ancestor of Edmund Randolph, first Attorney General of the United States, and of the immortal General Robert E. Lee. He added considerably to the original Poplar Neck holdings until the lands of Ripon Hall comprised 1,750 acres.

From the heirs of Edmund Jenings, Ripon Hall passed into the hands of the Carter family; first to Robert "King" Carter, one of the wealthiest and largest landholders in Virginia and later to his son, Landon Carter, who occupied the place at the time of the Revolution.

The adjoining 330 acres south of Ripon Hall Plantation were held by Robert Vaulx. "Vaulxland," as he called the estate, was patented in 1655; and on the north bank of the mouth of Queen's Creek, he built his manor house, Vaulx Hall. During the seventeenth and eighteenth centuries the property was successively the home of the Robert Vaulx, Peter Temple, George Richards, Samuel Timson, and Colonel Edward Champion Travis families. The point on which Vaulx Hall was built later became known as Timson Neck and Travis Point.

The land west of Camp Peary was owned by the Custis family. Daniel Parke Custis married Martha Dandridge and when Daniel died, his widow married George Washington.

One mile from the mouth of Queen's Creek, on the north side of the creek was Porto Bello, the country estate of Lord Dunmore, Royal Governor of the Virginia Colony at the outbreak of the Revolution.

Porto Bello had not been built by the Governor but was purchased from William Drummond in 1773 and used as a retreat and hunting lodge where Dunmore entertained many of the leading dignitaries of the times.

In spite of his sympathy with the cause of the coming Revolution, George Washington remained friendly with Lord Dunmore, and there is an entry in Washington's diary as late as May 26, 1774, that he rode out to have breakfast with the Governor at Porto Bello.

Upon receiving the news of the Battle of Lexington in April, 1775, and learning that the Virginia Militiamen were preparing to seize the arms and powder stored at Williamsburg, Lord Dunmore had the gunpowder removed to the man-of-war *Magdalen*. Arming his servants, he sent them from the Governor's Palace to Porto Bello and called for Captain Montagu of the man-of-war *Fowery*, then anchored in the York, to send up at midnight a detachment of marines and sailors to his assistance. These troops arrived at Porto Bello and the Governor made good his escape. This was the first outbreak of hostilities during the Revolution to take place in Virginia. When Dunmore fled the Virginia Colony the property of Porto Bello was seized by the newly formed government of the State of Virginia.

After six long years of war, the Revolution finally ended with the defeat and surrender of Cornwallis. One of the British Earl's outstanding officers, Lieutenant Colonel Tarleton, was bitter in denouncing the failure of Cornwallis to utilize Queen's Creek as an avenue for attacking Lafayette (then in Williamsburg) from the rear and thus destroying him before he could join Washington's forces and conduct the Siege of Yorktown.

During the War of 1812 privateers were fitted out in Queen's Creek but no military action is known to have taken place there, although British warships were reported to have been seen in the York. One account places the enemy at least twenty miles from Yorktown. This reference, dated July 2, 1813, was contained in a letter of some petulance from William Tazewell of Williamsburg to Governor Barbour:

> We have been for some days in a state of great consternation here. Not less than 14 of the enemy's Barges, accompanied by an armed brig

and 6 or 7 Tenders, have been engaged in the work of plundering and desolation in our immediate neighborhood. On yesterday evening, disgraceful to state, a party landed at Jas. Town, and after plundering the plantation, destroyed Lieut. Ambler's Household furniture of every description.

It has been estimated that, at the coming of the white man, the combined tribes of the Tidewater numbered about nine thousand Indians, all being of the Algonquin linguistic stock. Although illiterate, they nevertheless lived under an organized government, controlled by custom and tradition, which was made up of many districts or tribes, such as the Kiskiacks, each ruled over by a werowance or minor chief. In spite of their lack of mechanical devices, they were surprisingly adept in agricultural pursuits and before the white man came had domesticated more plants than any other race of men; namely, corn, rice, cotton, tobacco, coffee, potatoes, beans, peas, onions, pumpkins, and many others.

Besides their cultivated crops they had wild game, fish, oysters, berries, melons, and wild fruit for food. They pounded their corn into a meal which they mixed with water and made into hoe cakes and corn pone. Fire was made for cooking and warmth in the time honored manner of rubbing or twirling a dry, sharpened stick in contact with a hard wood block until the heat thus generated ignited the moss and dried leaves arranged about the contact point.

For shelter they built circular huts of boughs drawn and tied together at the top, the exterior being covered with bark and woven mats. Each such house sheltered a complete family that might number as many as twenty members. Apparently the houses or huts were identical in appearance and construction for Captain John Smith noted that "he who knoweth one such house knoweth them all." They had other rude structures for their religious rites wherein homage was paid to "evil favourably carved" images of their "okees" or gods. Medicine men or priests, grotesquely garbed, tended these places of worship.

The women wore rings, chains, shells, and beads for ornaments while the men went in for more original trappings, some having their ear lobes pierced and from the holes suspending "small green and yellow snakes . . . Others wore a Dead Rat tyed by the taile . . . he is the most gallant that is the most monstrous and uglie to behold." For dress

33

they depended upon the skins of animals ornamented with beads and painted designs, feather mantles, and a sort of cloth woven from grass. Both sexes painted and tattooed their faces and bodies with fanciful patterns and devices.

Although universally called "redskins," the Tidewater Indians were "of a colour browne when they are of any age but they are borne white," according to John Smith. Beards were not common and those Indians who wore them had one half shaven, the other long. They cut their black hair in many fashions but "ever some part remaineth long."

For amusement, when they were not engaged in the hunt or on the warpath, they played games of chance with sticks and pebbles, played games with a ball, smoked tobacco, sang, danced, and drank a liquor of their own manufacture until "they became sick." Smith wrote that they seldom made war for land or goods but principally for revenge. "They are inconstant in everything, soon mounted to anger, and so malicious that they seldom forget an injury."

Of the 1607 population of nine thousand Indians and a handful of English colonists only eight hundred Indian descendants exist today; whereas the present non-Indian population of Tidewater is over a million.

The most important and far reaching phase of the Indian life to affect the colonists was their tobacco culture. Columbus had returned from his first voyage with a strange tale of "smoking Indians," and Raleigh had brought some of the weed back to England in the sixteenth century. The French ambassador in Lisbon, Jean Nicot, had gained prominent interest in the plant throughout the continent when he had engaged the attention of Catherine de Medici by presenting her with a bundle of the leaves he had obtained from a sailor newly arrived from Virginia.

The use of tobacco was general among the Indians and their custom of making a solemn ceremony of their smoking circles caused the weed first to be called "Herba Sancta Indorum," the sacred Indian herb. It was their wont to squat glumly about a fire made of the dried leaves of a certain plant and inhale the smoke of that fire through hollow reeds called "tobaccoes" which they stuck in their nostrils, seemingly deriving no little pleasure from the effects thereof.

In Europe the apothecaries were prompt to exploit the new "drug" and, not having the slightest idea what it was, attributed to it marvelous healing powers. In one form or another, usually boiled for several hours into a tincture, it was prescribed to sufferers of widely differing complaints. At that, it probably possessed certain pharmaceutical authority for the patients either died on the spot or became encouraged to get better at once and avoid the possibility of a second dose.

The plant did not gain its tremendous popularity in Virginia until John Rolfe experimented with the growing of a milder Spanish variety of tobacco. While the hardy Indian, through long custom, was able to stomach the bitterness and bite of the native tobacco, it was much too vile to find smoking favor abroad. Rolfe discovered by experiment a method that made the tobacco sweet and pleasant to the taste when smoked in a clay pipe, producing a feeling of contentment and peace with the world, except in the case of small children who should have nothing to do with pipes, anyhow.

The new product met with such instantaneous success that overnight it found its way into the market, helping to fill the demand created when the tobacco craze spread all over Europe, until soon the whole world was smoking, snuffing and chewing tobacco. Money that the early colonists had begged for in vain for their colonizing ventures now came pouring out of England, and much of Virginia was laid bare for the planting of tobacco.

The original purpose of colonizing Virginia had been to "discover pearls and gold" and "to set up outposts against our ancient enemy, Spain," but these aims were forgotten in the unexpected wealth of the tobacco culture.

Advertisements exploiting the weed appearing in the periodicals and public places of the time were similar to the illustration shown, which has been called "America's first tobacco advertisement." Although the advertiser does not inform us how far the Indian depicted would walk for a twist of "Hogtail" or whether the "Common smoaking tobacco" had been toasted, fried or parboiled, the presentation of the advertisement is similar to some billboards we still see today. The Lorillard Company, which first published it many years ago, reprinted it as their contribution to the souvenir program of the Richmond Bicentennial celebration in 1937, and we include it here through their courtesy and the authorization of their agents, Lennen and Mitchell, Inc.

The tremendous increase in trade brought by the shipping of tobacco to and subsequent importing of articles from England and the Continent necessitated the creation of a series of ports along the Tidewater waterways. An Act for Ports, passed in 1691, required certain plantation owners, possessed of sites suitable for the purpose, to sell fifty acres of land each for use as town and port sites.

The little settlement at Kiskiack was suddenly roused to intense activity when Benjamin Read, who had inherited old grandfather Martiau's land below Kiskiack, was required to sell fifty acres of his land to establish a port at a point where the York River narrowed and where, from earliest times, there had always been a ferry to the Gloucester shore.

The new site was called Yorktown in honor of the Duke of York. So rapid was its growth and prosperity from the tobacco boom that within a very few years the Church, Courthouse, and other public activities which had heretofore been centered either at Kiskiack or the old settlement of Yorke, further down the river, were moved to Yorktown.

Tobacco & Snuff of the best quality & flavor,
At the Manufactory, No. 4, Chatham street, near the Gaol
By Peter and George Lorillard,
Where may be had as follows :

Cut tobacco,	Prig or carrot do.
Common kitefoot do.	Maccuba snuff,
Common smoaking do.	Rappee do.
Segars do.	Strasburgh do.
Ladies twist do.	Common rappee do.
Pigtail do. in small rolls,	Scented rappee do. of dif-
Plug do.	ferent kinds,
Hogtail do.	Scotch do.

The above Tobacco and Snuff will be sold reasonable, and warranted as good as any on the continent. If not found to prove good, any part of it may be returned, if not damaged.

1751
Loading Tobacco
at Yorktown, Virginia.

Yorktown

WHEN a Frenchman changes his nationality, that's news, and it was certainly good news to the Colony when the French military engineer, Captain Nicolas Martiau, after becoming naturalized by special proclamation of King James I, came out in 1620 to build forts in Virginia. A list of the "Living and Dead in Virginia" dated February 16, 1623, list "Cap. Nich Marteaw" as being among the living at "Elizabeth Cittie." Like so many seventeenth century names, Martiau was subjected to a variety of spellings. His patent of 1630 refers to him as "Martian" and another record alludes to him as Marcian. But because he signed himself "Martiau" and was so addressed in his correspondence from his patron, the Earl of Huntington, we shall confine ourselves to that spelling. "Captain Nick" was unrivalled in energy and application, and his feats of military prowess led him through operations of defense, offense, and romance.

In the former pursuits he directed the construction of the great log palisade between the headwaters of College and Queen Creeks and built the fort at York. He took the initiative in the offensive against his neighbor, Sir John Harvey, when that gentleman was guilty of misconducting the affairs of the Royal Governor's office. A year after arriving in the Colony, Captain Martiau became a member of the House of Burgesses at Jamestown and remained closely associated with that body for many years.

In 1624 he married Jane Berkeley, widow of young Leftenant Edward Berkeley who had been killed in the Indian massacre of 1622. Berkeley, a man of great industry, established the first iron works in America and would, no doubt, have made a real name for himself had not the Indians cut him down along with all of his iron-workers in a surprise attack. In marrying Jane, Martiau established himself and his family as the first ancestors in America of another eminent military engineer, George Washington. Good-wife Jane had a daughter, Jane, whom Martiau raised as one of his own.

The depredations of the Indians, climaxed by the 1622 uprising, had caused such concern among the first settlers that a series of forts and outposts were planned, and the first "western" frontier was established by a line crossing the Tidewater Peninsula from Jamestown to the Charles (York) River along which it was proposed to erect a wall of logs. The construction of this log palisade and the protective forts was entrusted to Martiau, and the site on the Charles selected for a fort was called York.

The fort at York occupied a point on the river at the mouth of Wormley Creek, named for the first settler in that section, Colonel Christopher Wormley, and lies about two miles down the river from the present site of Yorktown. The safety of the fort caused a settlement to spring up around it, and in 1633 York was selected as a receiving port. A store was built for receiving and shipping purposes, and to serve the inhabitants both of York and the settlement at Kiskiack.

So stoutly did Martiau build York fort that it was still in active use more than forty years later when it was described as "the most considerablest fortress in the country." During the Indian uprisings along the Rappahannock in 1676 the terror-stricken county folk of Gloucester fled across the river for refuge in the fort at York. They were dismayed to find that they could be afforded scant protection there, however, for to prevent the fort's stores of arms and ammunition falling into the hands of Nathaniel Bacon, who was also on the warpath, Governor Berkeley had taken them with him in his flight to the Eastern Shore.

Having engaged so actively in the defense against the Indians, it is reasonable to assume that Captain Martiau was eager to begin reaping some of the benefits to be derived from his own defensive works. He was also active in the legislative affairs of the Colony, as Representative in the House of Burgesses from both Kiskiack and the Isle of Kent in the Chesapeake, and he probably had a hand in framing the Court Order of October 8, 1630.

Captain Martiau was among the first settlers to qualify for land under this Act, following Captains Robert Felgate, John Utie, and John West into the wilderness of Kiskiack. For "the Adventure of himselfe, his wife and tenn persons to Chiskiake . . . and for the transportation at his own costs and charges of fourteene persons into this Colony," Governor Francis Wyatt granted Martiau patent to sixteen hundred acres on May 20, 1635, to be "augmented and doubled when he or his assigns shall have sufficiently peopled and planted the same." This land included the present site of Yorktown and lay between the holdings of Sir John Harvey who held patent to the land from directly east of Martiau to York at the mouth of Wormley Creek and the estate of Richard Townsend west of what is now Yorktown Creek.

Because of the tyrannical rule of neighbor Sir John Harvey during his term as Governor, Martiau strongly opposed him. Opposition, while general throughout the Colony, centered at York and Kiskiack, both being Burgess Districts separately represented in the Jamestown Assembly. It was daring of "Captain Nick" but typical of the man's spirit of fearless independence. If the campaign against Harvey had proven unsuccessful there is no doubt that Martiau would have lost favor with his patron in England, the Earl of Huntington, and his fortunes in Virginia would have come to a very definite ending. But Martiau was again fortunate. Governor Harvey was finally arrested by the colonists themselves and sent back to England.

The Harvey affair was one of the first manifestations of the strange new force of uncontrollable power at work in the minds of the first settlers. They tingled with unaccustomed impulses of freedom in this wild, new land; and for the first time, the united strength of the English yeomen seemed adequate to their imaginings. It was this unity of effort, while preserving the rights of the individual, that furthered their every activity.

In 1633 every fortieth man between the James and the York was directed to repair to the plantation of Dr. John Pott to be employed in building the houses of "Middle Plantation," that tiny budding settlement that was to blossom out into the City of Williamsburg and the Colonial Capital of Virginia. The men of York and Kiskiack can well be depended upon to have entered into the construction of Middle Plantation with the same energy and spirit with which they greeted each new enterprise.

The Legislature had divided Virginia into eight shires or counties in 1634, and Kiskiack and York had been included in Charles County which extended from beyond the Charles River to the center of the peninsula where it met James City County which, in its turn, included the land south to beyond the James River. Middle Plantation lay along the boundary dividing these two counties. In 1642 the name for both the river and county of Charles was changed to the York, in honor of the Duke of York who became James II, and the future site of Williamsburg found itself half in York County. The records of James City County were destroyed during the Civil War, but those of York County were preserved; and through their preservation, invaluable documentary research material for reference in the John D. Rockefeller restoration of the City of Williamsburg was provided.

Martiau was the most important of all the many Huguenots who increased the early population of the Colony, most of whom had been imported in order that the English settlers might "benefitt by the ffrenchmen's skill and instructinge of others in the Arte of plantinge and settinge of Vines and in the mistery of making Wyne."

"Captain Nick" scorned such puerile pursuits. He led expeditions against the Indians; continued to study and improve the colony's fortifications; brought many new immigrants to Virginia at his own expense; became a successful planter; was ever an active and vigilant protector of the people's rights in his legislative capacity in the Assembly; and became the First Citizen of the land that later was chosen for the site of Yorktown.

In fact, he might be called one of the Three Musketeers of seventeenth century American history; the other two being Captain John Smith of Jamestown and that other professional soldier, Captain Myles Standish of Plymouth. What a team these three would have made!

Besides his step-daughter, Jane, Martiau had four children of his own. His son, Nicolas Jr., died before reaching maturity. One daughter, Sarah, married Captain William Fuller, the Governor of Maryland. Another daughter, Mary, married Colonel John Scasbrook, a leader in the Bacon Rebellion. The third daughter, Elizabeth, married Colonel George Read who in 1637 was Secretary of the Colony and in 1638 was acting Governor. It is through Elizabeth and George Read that Washington traces his ancestry to Martiau, for the Read daughter, Mildred, married Augustine Warner II; the Warners' daughter, Mildred, married Lawrence Washington; the Washingtons' son, Augustine, married Mary Ball who was the mother of George Washington. Captain Nicolas Martiau thus became the great-great-great grandfather of the First President.

Washington himself appeared to be unacquainted with this foreign ancestor of his. In spite of the interest Washington's correspondence reveals concerning the genealogy of his family, his efforts centered on identifying the distinguished ancestors and kindred of the Washington name throughout English history; and in none of his writings on the subject does he at any time evince any knowledge of Nicolas Martiau, his French-Virginian ancestor.

Belated recognition was given the memory of "Captain Nick" in 1931 when a monument was dedicated in Yorktown to his everlasting glory. The dedication address was delivered by General John J. Pershing. The monument was designed by the eminent Philadelphia architect, Paul Cret, and consists of an eleven-foot shaft of Vermont granite bearing a bronze tablet with this inscription under the Grand Cross of the Huguenots:

SITE OF THE HOME OF

NICOLAS MARTIAU

THE ADVENTUROUS HUGUENOT

HE WAS BORN IN FRANCE 1591

CAME TO VIRGINIA 1620

AND DIED AT YORKTOWN 1657.

HE WAS A CAPTAIN IN THE INDIAN UPRISING

A MEMBER OF THE HOUSE OF BURGESSES

JUSTICE OF THE COURT OF YORK

IN 1635 A LEADER

IN THE THRUSTING OUT OF GOVERNOR HARVEY

WHICH WAS THE FIRST OPPOSITION

IN THE BRITISH COLONIAL POLICY.

THE ORIGINAL PATENTEE FOR YORKTOWN

AND THROUGH THE MARRIAGE

OF HIS DAUGHTER ELIZABETH

TO COL. GEORGE READ HE BECAME

THE EARLIEST AMERICAN ANCESTOR OF BOTH

GEN. GEORGE WASHINGTON

AND GOVERNOR THOMAS NELSON.

Marked by

the Huguenot Society of Pennsylvania

in coöperation with the National Federation

of Huguenot Societies and the Yorktown

Sesqui-Centennial Commission.

1931

As Yorktown was not established until 1691 it was a neat chronological trick for "Captain Nick" to have died there in 1657, but perhaps this is "straining at gnats."

A fact that does invite notice in passing, however, is that the monument marking the "site" of Martiau's home is on Lot No. 16 of Ballard Street. When Martiau's grandson, Benjamin Read, sold part of the old Martiau Plantation in 1691 to the Crown as the site for Yorktown he retained Lot No. 5 of Buckner Street. Is it not likely that he thus retained the old homesite? An incident supporting this supposition was the finding on Lot No. 5 of the tombstones of Martiau's daughter, Elizabeth, and her husband, Colonel George Read. These stones were dug up when Buckner Street was regraded and were removed to Grace Episcopal Churchyard.

In 1936 a new water line was laid down along Buckner Street and the necessary trenching revealed eighteen ancient burials on Lot No. 5. None of the graves were identified and as the water lines, like the U. S. Mail, "must go through" the remains were unceremoniously moved to the opposite side of the street.

The burial place of Captain Nicolas Martiau has never been located. Is it not possible that he would have been buried, as was the custom of the time, in his own burial ground upon his own land? Perhaps among those unmarked graves on Buckner Street in Yorktown, rudely disturbed from his original interment, uneasily lies "Captain Nick," the first American ancestor of that immortal personage, General George Washington.

Support might be added to the selection of Lot No. 16 as the Martiau home site if the custom had been to place the family burial plots behind the house, but in the majority of cases, the burying grounds were placed in front of the house. As the highest elevation was usually selected for the plantation house, and the site of the Read graves has already been established, it is possible that the Martiau monument should have been placed west rather than east of Buckner Street.

Elizabeth, daughter of Captain Nicolas Martiau, inherited her father's plantation and on her death it passed to her son, Benjamin Read. "Captain Nick" had lived to see the tobacco culture, started from most unpretentious beginnings, become the major industry of the Colony.

In 1662 a law was passed ordering that four towns be built to serve as ports of entry and shipping, one on the York, one on the Rappahannock, one on the Potomac, and the other on the Eastern Shore; but nothing tangible came of this legislation. In 1680 a still more extensive program of town building was ordered that selected eighteen sites throughout Tidewater and included the Read Plantation in York County, but again there was no active response because the law did not provide funds to purchase land and none of the planters owning the selected sites took the initiative in building at their own expense.

Finally, in 1691, an Act for Ports provided for the purchase of tracts of land in certain specified places along the Tidewater waterways for the building of port towns through which all imports and exports were required to pass and included ". . . that for the better securing of all tobaccoes, goods, wares and mechandises, which shall be brought to and landed at the ports . . . the surveyor of each county lay out and survey fifty acres of land . . . for the ports, wharfes, erecting warehouses or any other houses . . ." The place specified in the Act "ffor Yorke County, was to be upon Mr. Benjamin Reade's land beginning at the lower side of Smith's Creeks, and so running downward by the river towards the fferrey."

The ferry mentioned must have ceased operation subsequently for on November 7, 1705, the House of Burgesses concerned itself with a "grievance from York County Complaining That There is no ferry kept in York Town." A bill was accordingly prepared providing that a ferry be constantly kept from Yorktown to Tindal's Point on the Gloucester shore; the fare to be seven pence halfpenny for a man and fifteen pence for a man and horse. That the ferry was in active operation throughout the eighteenth century is testified to by an advertisement of 1769 appearing in the Williamsburg *Gazette* stating that the ferry to the York side:

> . . . is now kept by the subscriber: who hereby informs the public that he keeps as good boats and hands as can be found at any ferry in the Colony; and where all Gentlemen, Travellers and others, may be assured of meeting with a quick passage, as he will make it his study to render everything as agreeable as he possibly can.
>
> THOMAS HARWOOD

Major Lawrence Smith, the Indian fighter and one of Berkeley's staunch supporters against Bacon the Rebel, was also Surveyor for the County of York. He did "lay out and survey" the fifty-acre tract into the eighty-five lots of half-acre each along the seven streets of Yorktown that maintain their original lines to this day.

A single, principal street parallels the river at the top of the bluff overlooking the water and is called Main Street, running in a northwest and southeast direction. All the other seven streets intersect Main Street at right angles and run northeast and southwest. Starting at the western end of town and traveling east they are Buckner, Ballard, Church, Read, Nelson, Smith, and Bacon Streets. After the Revolution an eighth intersecting street was formed and called Comte de Grasse Street in honor of the commander of the French fleet.

The fifty acres thus surveyed by Smith at the Great Bend of the York were purchased from Read for ten thousand pounds of tobacco but did not include a strip of five acres between the town site and the river which was left "for a common shore of no value." This strip, of apparently no value in 1691, became very much of value in 1738 by which time so many disputes had risen as to the rights and title to this particular strip of shore that another Act was passed to remedy the defect of the first Act and providing for the purchase of the land from the heirs of Benjamin Read who claimed title to it. "It is plain," read the Act of 1738, "that the fifty acres laid out for a port and town . . . ought to have been laid off next and adjoining to the river . . ." Lawrence Smith, who had laid out the original fifty acres, was again engaged to set up his instrument and survey this five-acre strip between the town and the low water mark of the river, and the land was declared to be a commons for the use of the town inhabitants "from henceforth, for ever." Forever, in this case, meant until 1785 when part of the commons was subdivided and sixty-four new lots were added to the eighty-five of the original 1691 survey. The remaining portion of the commons was held by the Town Trustees for one hundred and fifty years until it was turned over to the United States Government in 1934 as a part of Colonial National Historical Park.

Of the manner in which the first wharves at Yorktown were constructed we have no definite account, but we may logically assume that they were built of logs very similar to those of the same period and purpose at Norfolk. William Byrd has described their construction in his writings of 1728: "The wharfs were built with Pine Logs let into each other at the End, by which those underneath are made firm by those which lye over them" and again, "The method of building Wharffs here is after the following manner. They lay down long Pine Logs. . . . These are bound fast together by Cross-Pieces notcht into them, according to the Architecture of the Log-Houses in North Carolina. A Wharff built thus will stand several years, in spight of the Worm, which bites here very much, but may be soon repaired in a Place where so many Pines grow in the Neighborhood."

These repairs were necessary not only because of the damage caused by "vast Beds of Seedling-worms, which by degrees eat the Plank into cells like those of a Honeycomb," but also by the "ruinous condition, occasioned chiefly by ships, and other vessels heaving down by and mooring at the wharf." During certain years storms and "great freshets" also damaged the river front and there is record of one wharf which was "carried away by the Gust in 1774." The York River is still subject to these disastrous weather conditions; in August, 1933, a severe storm and high turbulent waters carried away practically everything along the river below Yorktown.

45

The sketch heading this chapter was based upon a similar scene depicted in an engraving that embellishes the Fry and Jefferson map of Virginia, first published in 1751. Evidently this scene, showing a corner of the warehouse together with part of the wharf; a group of planters, inspectors, slaves and workers; and ships riding at anchor in the river harbor, was considered quite typical of the waterfront and the tobacco industry, for it is faithfully repeated in later editions of the map published in 1755 and 1775.

Many wharves were built along the "common shore" to accommodate the growing trade and shipping. Besides the private wharves, warehouses, cranes, chandlers, grog-shops, and other typical waterfront structures, Yorktown itself maintained a "Publick Wharf," conditioned and supported by the public monies. Charles Chiswell was granted patent to a parcel of land along the river to erect a warehouse and wharf "for his greater Conveniency in Victualing His Majesty's Ships of War according to his Contract made with the Commanders of the Victualing Office." Among the town merchants whose warehouses crowded the shore below the town was Cole Digges, builder and owner of a "commodious Warehouse and Wharf" which he built in 1729 "for the more Convenience in Landing Merchandise."

The warehouses were sometimes called "rolling-houses" because of the manner in which the tobacco was brought to them. After curing, the tobacco leaves were placed in huge hogsheads, an axle run through the center and engaged to a shaft on either side of which oxen were yoked, and the hogsheads were thus rolled from the plantations to the shipping points and warehouses.

In order to protect the contents of the "rolls," tobacco rolling was done in the late summer when the roads were dry. Consequently the summer was the busiest season for the river-front and during that period, like ancient Troy, Yorktown became a walled city. But hers was a wall of ships, turreted by the tall spars of the merchantmen and men-of-war.

The size of the tobacco hogsheads or casks was fixed by law, the inside diameter of the cask head being thirty inches and the staves forty-eight inches long. Ships used in the tobacco trade were built to accommodate casks of this size, and the holds were designed to carry seven tiers of casks.

46

The importance of Yorktown as a tobacco port was such that the House of Burgesses provided for the constant attendance of Tobacco Inspectors at the Yorktown warehouses so that there would be no delay in loading and unloading the ships. A further Act of the General Assembly in 1734 stipulated that "if at any of the warehouses there shall not be sufficient room for the receiving and securing of tobacco, the county courts shall order other necessary houses to be built . . . and if the owners shall refuse to do it, the same shall be done at the charge of the County"; in short, nothing was to be allowed to interfere in any way with the prosperous tobacco trade.

And prosperous it certainly was. The new town blossomed into a thriving village, and within a very few years all eighty-five of the town lots had been purchased and built upon. Fifty years after its founding Yorktown was doing a business, the exports alone of which amounted to £32,000 annually.

The tobacco fleet brought back from England fineries and luxuries from the shops of Bristol, Plymouth, and London; silks, satins, and laces from the Continent; bonnets and gloves, gowns and cloaks of the current mode; jewelry and silver plate in the popular patterns; wines and brandies; riding gear and glittering coaches; swords and firearms; fine furniture of mahogany; lutes, spinets, and harpsichords; books both classical and of the moment; all the merchandise that a moneyed and leisurely class made possible. It was the hey-day of the Virginia Colony, and the people of Yorktown generously shared in this good fortune that was so evident everywhere.

Let us consider what manner of folks were these good people of Yorktown. The popular theory that Virginia became peopled during the seventeenth century by a courtly, *distingue* group of aristocratic sophisticates known as Cavaliers has been very satisfactorily disputed by the eminent Professor Thomas Jefferson Wertenbaker of Princeton, who wrote:

> My studies lead me to the conclusion . . . that the Colonial aristocracy was created in Virginia and not transplanted from England. Obviously, the Virginia aristocracy was of mixed origin; some no doubt counting among their ancestors here and there a man of rank and distinction; some coming directly from the gentry or mercantile class; some being self-made men who worked their way up from the lower classes. But I have found

47

no evidence of any large migration of aristocrats, or so-called Cavaliers. The Virginia aristocrat as we know him was, in my opinion, chiefly the product of the tobacco plantation and not merely an English aristocrat living in Virginia.

The expansive and lordly plantation life that has all too often been attributed to the participants having been accustomed to such aristocratic delights in England was of no such basis. This mode and manner of living was occasioned merely by the fact that many tobacco farmers and small merchants suddenly found themselves tremendously wealthy through enormously increased demands for their crops and markets for their wares.

They thereupon did what any sensible person does with money — spent it. And if in spending it they built magnificent houses bordered by lovely gardens; gave brilliant balls and entertainments; gambled for high stakes and indulged prodigiously in fermented spirits; went about elegantly appareled; attended Church and attained high offices of public trust and honor; it by no means followed that these lordly traits and customs were bred from an aristocratic lineage. It merely meant that, as a class, the tobacco planters and merchants of Virginia were men of sound sense and admirable taste and had the money to defend the former and indulge the latter.

Like every other group of wealth and power throughout history, the great plantation owners soon established an aristocracy of their own in Virginia. This, of course, does not mean that every Englishman who ventured to the Colony, or every Virginian who was born there, was blessed with good fortune and abundance. The successful planters and the successful merchants formed a very limited minority at the top of a social and economic pyramid that broadened out into groups or classes of ever increasing numbers as it descended down through the small propertied yeoman, the small unsuccessful merchants, the overseers and tenant farmers, the bond or indentured servants, and finally, the slaves by whose labor the leisure of the planter was made possible. All of these varied social levels were represented among the population of Yorktown.

Plantations hemmed the town which had been created from plantation acres and were bordered by even greater plantations that reached to the James. Across the York each "neck" in Gloucester held the

48

manor house of a prosperous tobacco planter, and everyone of these individuals was well-known in the busy streets of Yorktown. At Williamsburg, which succeeded Jamestown as the capital of Virginia in 1699, the gay and brilliant Court season brought those of wealth and culture from all the Colony; and in their periodic peregrinations to and from the Capital City, much of the traffic was borne by the Yorktown Road and the Yorktown ferry.

The citizenry of York was united by birth and marriage with all of the great families throughout Virginia, and as a town of Tidewater, Yorktown knew on intimate terms the mighty ones thereof, following their careers and sharing in their economic and political fortunes. From among these mighties of Tidewater were to come in later years five of the first ten presidents of the United States: Washington, Madison, Monroe, Harrison, and Tyler while a sixth, Jefferson, spent a large part of his active life there. Thomas Nelson, a native of Yorktown and son of the Tidewater, became the third governor of Virginia after it had become a state.

An outstanding feature of those whose names were prominent in the Colony's early days was their youth. To mention but a few, there were Captain Nicolas Martiau, already a famous engineer at twenty-nine; Captain John Smith, only twenty-eight; and Major Gooch who died at twenty-nine. Edward Digges became Governor at thirty, and Alexander Spotswood at thirty-four; Lafayette, the boy general, was only twenty-one, and the great Washington was a commissioned surveyor at seventeen! At an age when the modern youth is struggling for a foothold on the bottom rung of the ladder these men of the seventeenth and eighteenth centuries had already reached the top and were making history.

The almost universal prevalence of military titles among the gentry was occasioned by legislation that made every male of military age subject to militia duty, exceptions being made for servants and slaves. All holders of official positions, in order to preserve the dignity of their respective offices, were exempt from the monthly company and annual general musters of the militia but were required to provide themselves with arms and horses and were liable, in time of danger, for services as officers "in such stations as are suitable for gentlemen." This practice of excusing the ranking officers from the appointed drills met with not only the approval of the planters most concerned, but also found favor with the growing feeling of independence among the rank and file of the militia. What cared they if not one of their officers had the benefit of an army training? They thought this preferable to having "an Adjutant in every neck to huff and bully ye people . . . and govern Arbitrarily and by Martial Law."

As practically every plantation owner of any consequence was also holder of an official position in the affairs of the Colony, he thereby automatically became an officer in the militia; hence, the long list of Captains, Majors, and Colonels to be found among our early Yorktown friends.

Many of the Yorktown residents were also plantation owners and maintained their town houses in style and elegance. An English visitor describing the town in 1764 remarked, "You perceive a great air of opulence amongst the inhabitants . . . every considerable man keeps an equipage . . . There are some very pretty garden spots in the town; and the avenues leading to Williamsburg and Norfolk are prodigiously agreeable. The roads are infinitely superior to most in England. The country surrounding is thickly overspread with plantations, and the planters live in a manner equal to men of the best fortune."

The society of this upper stratum of the early Virginia social structure was largely that of a city people transferred to unaccustomed rural conditions. It was composed of men and women of culture and education and, as a class, was perhaps the most enlightened set of immigrants ever to have settled a new country. Because of the economic structure of the plantation existence most of them lived, community life was limited but social contacts were encouraged by meetings during sessions of the County Court at Yorktown, the Assembly at Williamsburg, balls, horse races, marriages and funerals, and the never ending visiting between plantations.

To understand the tremendous flow of the laboring element that made up the larger part of the early population in Virginia, we may be permitted to digress a bit. This element was comprised of four classes: the bonded or indentured servant, the runaway seaman, the transported convict, and the slave. We will attempt to outline briefly the conditions that made them leave the known conditions of their homes, however hard, to accept the equal hardships of the unknown Virginia wilderness.

The sudden and unexpected deluge of gold and silver that came from South America by way of Spain and Portugal and flooded all of western Europe for the preceding century had also, in the peculiar manner which great wealth has, affiliated itself with a small number of merchants and princes. Seeking an avenue by which this wealth might be invested at a profit, a considerable part of it was directed back in the direction from whence it came, to increase the fortunes of the American colonies.

At the same time, the immense holdings of the Church had been confiscated by the Government; hundreds of thousands of people who, by their labors, had tilled the fields and supported the enterprises of the monastic establishments were thus deprived of their livelihood and were placed among the unemployed.

There was no place for them in the Old Country, but the industry being created by invested wealth in the New World demanded labor, and thousands of the working classes had become so poor and wretched that they were willing to go anywhere, even to the ends of the terrible Virginia wilderness, if they could relieve the distress and hopelessness of their condition at home.

Thus they became ready and willing subscribers to the system of indenture that required years of enforced labor in the Virginia Colony but held out as a reward ultimate freedom and the opportunity to obtain land of their own. Most such workers were indentured or bonded for seven years, but if they were very young their indenture was set until they had reached their twenty-fourth year, for both men and women.

These bonded servants immigrated by the boatload to be sold to the highest bidder for their seven or more years of service.

When so many of the inhabitants of England were willing to work out their passage to Virginia by as much as seven years of labor, it is not strange that seamen deserted their ships in American waters, thus to obtain their passage at no greater price than the forfeiture of pay for the outward voyage. Both merchantmen and men-of-war became so handicapped by such desertions that it became necessary for Governor Spotswood to issue a proclamation in 1710 forbidding the harboring of seamen who could not give a good account of themselves. It also required shipmasters who made Yorktown a port of call and all the officers of the Colony to arrest straggling seamen and clap them in irons on board the warships. Rewards of £5 were paid informers whose testimony resulted in the conviction of anyone harboring deserting sailors, and constables who permitted their escape were fined five hundred pounds of tobacco.

In spite of these drastic measures seamen continued to desert their ships, in fact were aided by the planters who thus obtained labor without the expense of paying the transportation of indentured servants. As the trade and shipping increased, the population of the colony became more and more enlarged by the desertions of the seamen, and ships deserted at Yorktown became an increasing problem.

The policy of England to ship her criminals to the colonies had from the first met with little favor in Virginia, but all efforts of the Colony to stop this traffic were nullified by the British authorities. As a matter of fact, those transported were not all necessarily hardened criminals. The penal code of England at that time punished most serious crimes with the gallows and those sent to Virginia were, in the main, political prisoners, debtors, or victims of economic or arbitrary laws of the time.

To the complaints of the colonists against this wholesale transportation of a criminal class, regardless of its quality, the contractors engaged in the lucrative trade replied that to stop the traffic would ruin their business. An Act of 1722, in which the Colony attempted to prevent convicts from entering Virginia, was disallowed by England upon petition from the contractors.

At the base of the economic pyramid, in Yorktown as throughout the Colony, were the slaves.

Slavery had existed in America long before the white men came. The practice of forced servitude had long been established by the Indians who enslaved their captives. It was almost natural for the early settlers, therefore, to enslave the Indians. But the Indians, thus reduced, would not work or in any other way co-operate with the desires of their white masters. When Robert Boyle, the celebrated natural philosopher, endowed William and Mary College with £200 to educate Indian children, the tribes willingly sent their prize offspring to the school. But when the "tributaries," or all those tribes who recognized the authority of the Colonial government, discovered that the children they had sent to Williamsburg to become scholars had been sold as slaves, they re-

52

fused to continue the arrangement and Brafferton Hall ceased to function as an Indian "school."

The advent of the African Negro into the Colony met immediately the demand for wholesale unskilled labor. The bond servants, escaped sailors, and transported convicts did very well for the various semi-skilled trades but were wholly unsuited for the field work of the plantation. In order to maintain profits the planter had to keep down the cost of production by cultivating on a large scale with the cheapest labor: the African Negro. In the first quarter of the eighteenth century alone, over twenty thousand Negro slaves were brought to Virginia, and many of them first set foot on American soil at Yorktown. As a man's wealth became known by the number of pounds of tobacco he could command, so the size of his plantation was judged by the number of slaves he owned.

The slave trade was a most profitable business, and a Yorktown merchant, when proposing a partnership in importing slaves, wrote in 1750: "There is not the least fear of selling here, for there is in general as many Purchases as there is slaves imported, and the pay is always better than for any other commodity."

Tobacco had become not only the staple product of Virginia but the accepted medium of exchange and was legal tender, according to weight, for most public or private debts. Since it was subject to fluctuations in price, and price varied according to quality, it was not a very satisfactory currency. While a man's fortune or an article's worth was counted in pounds of tobacco, there still circulated among the shops some ready cash in English money and Spanish pistoles or "p'cs of 8/8 (pieces of eight) w'ch is the common currency of these colonys." Virginia was still using Spanish dollars in the last quarter of the eighteenth century.

Virginia, a young community in which land was plentiful, grew rapidly during the early eighteenth century. In 1702 the number of those subject to the poll tax (titheables) was 25,099. By 1724 it had grown to 43,877, an increase of 75 per cent in twenty-two years for the Colony at large and 150 per cent for the area around Yorktown.

All land between the York and the James not swamp or waste land had been patented early. From 1725 on the increase in population was taken up in the frontier counties to the west, and according to the

Carolina charter of 1665, the boundary between Virginia and Carolina counties extended "west in a direct line, as far as the South seas"— modestly stopping short of the Pacific Ocean and the Orient!

The greatest attraction of the West lay in its unexploited land suitable for the growing of tobacco. Already the broad acres of the Tidewater were becoming exhausted because large crops were necessary to maintain the high standard of living that had been set, and the restricted lands between the rivers would not allow for large acreage lying fallow. However, if any lordly planter of Tidewater gave passing thought to the impending disaster that soil exhaustion was sure to bring, he gave it no serious consideration. He was riding the wave of prosperity while it lasted and was determined to enjoy it to the full.

Then came the downward swing of the pendulum. Worn out soil began to produce poor and scanty crops. Inferior tobacco brought low prices. Small crops meant small incomes, and to complete the vicious circle, small incomes brought about a falling off of taxes. The same conditions prevailed also in Maryland and the Carolinas.

Purchasing of slaves to the limit of their credit had plunged the planters into debts that were no longer justified by the results of their crops. To increase prices, laws were passed reducing the size of tobacco crops by forbidding the tending of "seconds" (the sprouting growing on the plants after the crop had been gathered). Fines of five hundred pounds of tobacco were levied against every titheable employed on an offending plantation, without curbing this practice.

The mad bustle that Yorktown had known at the height of the tobacco boom began to slacken, and the business of the port resolved itself into a steady, less spectacular but more solid, flow of normal trade.

How long it would have lasted as a commercial town had not the Revolution brought the Siege of 1781, and with it the cessation of all business, is hard to say. The rivers were no longer the main arteries of travel, new roads were webbing the land; and with the changing centers of population, Yorktown no longer enjoyed its key position as a principal port.

The wealth of the surrounding plantations diminished with the poverty of the land, and it may well have been that the Siege actually administered the *coup de grace* to an already slowly dying town.

The story of the Siege is related in some detail in a later chapter.

Its devastating effect, from which Yorktown never recovered, was described a few days after the surrender of Cornwallis by the Abbe Robin, chaplain with Lafayette's troops:

> I have been through the unfortunate little town of York since the siege, and saw many elegant houses shot through and through in a thousand places, and ready to crumble to pieces; rich household furniture crushed under their ruins, or broken by the brutal English soldier; carcases of men and horses half covered with dirt; books piled in heaps, and scattered among the ruins of the buildings . . .

The depredations of the "brutal English soldier" were not alone responsible for the deplorable conditions of the town. The long occupation of the Virginia Militia had reduced many of the deserted dwellings in which the troops were billeted to a shambles; the fences, outbuildings, and even furniture having fed their winter fires. Long unpaid, the soldiers had pillaged and ransacked every available source of booty. Most citizens who fled the town had been unable to remove their valuables and lost all their possessions. As early as 1776, claims for damages were being pressed against the Militia.

The Surrender had brought Yorktown immortality, but at a price that left it damaged almost beyond revival. Between the Sieges of 1781 and 1862 the only occurrence of note that marked the crippled hamlet was the great conflagration of 1814 which laid waste many of the more substantial houses that had weathered the 1781 Siege. The riverfront was ravaged by this fire, and the only structure of the Colonial period that survives below the town today is the Archer Cottage, one of the simple frame dwellings that had been built along the waterfront in the early days.

The occupation and Siege of 1862 is treated elsewhere in this volume, and a mention of the Centennial recognition of Yorktown in 1881 is accounted for in the chapters devoted to the Moore House and the Victory Monument.

During the First World War, the Chesapeake Bay and the York River were used as a base for the Atlantic Fleet. The fuel oil station for the Fifth Naval District was established immediately below Yorktown on land of old Temple Farm. This has since become the U.S. Coast Guard Reserve Training Center. The broad acres of Kiskiack, Bellfield, and Ringfield became the Navy Mine Depot, later to be expanded as the Naval Weapons Station. Today Yorktown would indeed be sore pressed to justify its continued existence, were it not for its still vividly remembered glorious past.

The importance of that past has long been appreciated by individuals and patriotic organizations who have done much to make manifest the possibilities which Yorktown, Williamsburg, and Jamestown offered. This sentiment has culminated in a movement to create a historical area in Virginia which would include Yorktown, Williamsburg, Jamestown, and Gloucester Point. A bill establishing these areas as Colonial National Monument, introduced by Congressman Louis C. Cramton, of Michigan, was approved by President Hoover on December 30, 1930. The government has acquired, including Jamestown Island, more than 7,000 acres in and around Yorktown.

The name of the national monument was changed in 1936 to Colonial National Historic Park. Today the Park, as a public reservation, interprets the true significance of Yorktown as a vital factor in the life of the Virginia Colony and as the birthplace of American Independence. The annual celebration of the surrender of Cornwallis on "Yorktown Day," October 19th, has become an affair of national importance.

It is strange that the history of the Colonial period should have reached its consummation at Yorktown only twenty miles from its beginning at Jamestown. Yet, on the small peninsula that separates these two historic spots, many of the scenes making up that history were enacted.

Grace Episcopal Church

MILLIONS of years ago the ocean covered all of the Tidewater country, and the peninsula between the York and the James was part of the ocean floor. Countless generations of oysters, clams and scallops, depositing their shells, built the floor higher and higher. Then came the run-off of the water and the emergence of the land around the Chesapeake. A deep depression between the York and Gloucester shores became the long, narrow tidal inlet we call the York River. The continual ebb and flow of the river's tide has worn away the high banks just below Yorktown revealing the layer on layer of shells mixed with the muck and clay of the former ocean bottom. The action of the lime in the decomposing shells, in composition with the clay, formed a dense, rocky substance known as marl. Where the marl remains under water along the river it is soft and at low tide is easily dug from the banks. After a few weeks' exposure to sun and air, however, the lime crystallizes and sets up into a stonelike hardness.

The early settlers at Yorktown found this material very suitable for certain building purposes; it was used in many of the foundations of the first buildings, and a few were built entirely of marl.

The old York-Hampton Church (now the Grace Episcopal

Church) is one such structure. Perched high on its marl bluff overlooking the river, this ancient house of worship has witnessed and withstood all of the trials and tribulations that reduced Yorktown from a thriving town to an almost forgotten, scattered remnant of its former self. The little chapel seems to have taken unto itself the eternal qualities of the cliff above which it stands and the material from which it was built. Burned, desecrated, altered and repaired, but never completely abandoned, the church has come through its viscissitudes to be rebuilt ever stronger and each time more firmly placed in the hearts of those who worship within its walls.

About six years after the founding of Yorktown the church was built upon its present site. A year before "on Oct. ye 26th, 1696" the Royal Governor, Francis Nicholson, had lent stimulus to the building venture by addressing the following letter to the York County Court, "I promise to give five pounds sterl. towards building, the Cort house att Yorke Town. And twenty pounds sterl. if within two years they build a brick church att ye same Town. . ."

The church was built, but of marl instead of brick. The Governor apparently considered that his handsome contribution to the building fund entitled him to certain considerations for we find him cursing in high rage a few years later because burial fees were asked for the interment of one of his friends, Captain Nevill. Nevill commanded the man-of-war guarding the tobacco fleet and the capes. He died on September 11, 1701, on board his ship *Lincoln* and was brought to Yorktown for burial.

> The next morning the Governor desired . . . to go to York . . . to Capt. Nevill's burial, who had been dead three or four days — the corpse being in ye ground but not covered. There was a sermon preached by the Chaplain of the Ship *Lincoln*. The sermon being over, as also the ceremony, (the writer) went out of the church where he saw and heard ye Governor swearing ye most horrid oaths — upon enquiring ye reason — the answer was made — that it was because Slaughter (the Parish minister) had asked some fees of some of the officers of the *Lincoln* for burying Capt. Nevill in the Church.

Prior to the building of the Yorktown Church, religious services were held in the churches at the earlier parishes of York on Wormley

Creek, Charles on the Poquosson River, and at Kiskiack eight miles above Yorktown. The silver communion service still used in Grace Episcopal Church was supposedly a gift from Queen Anne to the Kiskiack church. The hallmark shows it to have been made in 1649 and it is engraved: "Hampton Parish in Yorke County, Virginia." The service, which was transferred to Yorktown when the Hampton Parish church fell into disuse, consists of two silver pieces, a flagon 10¼ inches high and a cup 8½ inches.

With the abandonment of old Yorke and the removal of the county seat to the new village of Yorktown, the little marl church on the bluff became the center of religious worship for both Yorke and Hampton Parishes for ". . . to this busy emporium of trade, the courthouse and church were transferred." Nothing now remains of the first church at Yorke Parish, which was built in 1642, except a section of the foundation wall; the entire town, which was the county seat until around 1680, has disappeared. Within the early church foundations is a grave site covered by a tombstone bearing the name of Major William Gooch and the date of his death, 1655. Although Gooch was only twenty-nine when he died, he had already been a member of the King's Council and represented York County in the House of Burgesses in 1654. His tombstone is the oldest in York County and one of the oldest in Virginia. Local legend avows that Governor Alexander Spotswood also lies interred near this spot, but this is hardly probable even though the exact place of his burial never has been learned. In 1845 William Sheild, who at one time owned the property, wrote Bishop Meade that, ten years previous to his writing, a pile of broken tombstone fragments had been found at the site of the old York church, one of which bore the letters of Spotswood's name. In the chapter relating to the Moore House this dissertation is treated at greater length.

From the very first, the new church at Yorktown was ably supported, and during the first half of the eighteenth century the vestry and congregation would not have suffered for elegance and gentility by comparison with those of the much larger Bruton Parish in Williamsburg.

Clergymen were in great demand, and twenty pounds were offered to anyone who should import a minister into the Colony. Ministers, with six servants each, were exempt from taxes and the twentieth "calfe, kidd of goats and piggs" and tithes of tobacco were imposed to support the clergy.

The citizens of Yorktown, in common with all the people of the Virginia Colony, identified themselves with the Church as they identified themselves with the Government. They were the Church as they were the State. As they built and furnished their churches out of their own means, they naturally contended they were the owners thereof. The vestry was elected by the people, and the clergy were appointed by the vestry with clearly defined duties and authority. As representatives of the people, the vestry demanded a high standard of life and character on the part of the clergy. In the event of any improper behavior, a clergyman was summoned before the vestry and tried; if the charges were proven he was expelled.

The first rector of the combined York and Hampton parishes was the Reverend Anthony Panton. For criticizing and calling the Secretary of the Colony a "jackanapes," Panton was relieved of his charge. The early history of the Yorktown church is marked by constant change among its clergy and involvements in disputes between the Governor and the vestries and the restless church element of Williamsburg. The Parish, however, continued to thrive. In his report of 1724 to the Bishop of London, the Reverend Francis Fontaine speaks of his Yorktown flock thus: "My parish is twenty miles in length and four miles broad. There are two hundred families in it. In my church at Yorktown there are three score communicants."

The York-Hampton Parish was one of the most sought after appointments in Virginia, and many men of solid worth and prominence in the Church occupied its pulpit. The Reverend John Cramm, while minister of York-Hampton, led the organized clergy in their attempt to persuade the Royal Governor to amend the King's laws pertaining to remuneration of the clergy. After the Reverend Cramm the church was shepherded by a gentleman of evangelical inclinations and great oratorical powers. He was the Reverend Mr. Sheild and, although a certain element of his congregation considered him "rather too much of a Methodist," he preached to a well-filled church. "At a time when stiff brocades were the church dress of those who could afford it," we are told, "a lady would come home after some of Mr. Sheild's more animated discourses and call upon her maid to take off her clothes, for she had heard so much of Hell, Damnation and Death that it would take her all the evening to get cool."

The church continued to enjoy the good fortunes of the town until the dark clouds of the Revolution brought the British occupation in 1781, and then indeed hard days befell it. Cornwallis was delighted to find so staunch a depository for his gunpowder; the pews and church furniture were ruthlessly destroyed while the stout marl walls were made to serve as a powder magazine. York County records of the time state, "The windows and pews having been broken and destroyed and the Church used as a magazine the damages were valued at £150. The destruction was wrought by Lord Cornwallis." It may have been this desecration of sacred property that in later years influenced the Reverend Scervant Jones, one-time proprietor of the Swan Tavern in Yorktown, to even matters by preaching to his Baptist flock in the old Powder Horn at Williamsburg, the magazine and armory of the Royal Governors.

After the Siege had terminated in the surrender of Cornwallis, loving hands labored to erase the scars of war from the building, and the church was once more devoted to its rightful purpose. But York was no longer the desirable parish it had been before the Revolution— the old families deserted it; the inhabitants around connected themselves with other denominations. Even in its reduced state the church was not to enjoy the blessings of a peaceful life for many years, because in the great conflagration that destroyed half the town in 1814, the church was badly burned. The story has persisted for many years that the burning of Yorktown was occasioned by "marauding British soldiers," but there is no official record of the British fleet ever coming up the York. Their objective was Washington, and upon leaving the Chesapeake they proceeded directly up the Potomac.

Apparently York-Hampton Church had not yet been rebuilt ten years after the 1814 fire, for Bishop Moore preached in the Courthouse and in Mr. Nelson's house in 1825; and in the same year, the Reverend Mark Chevers reported that he had "for some months past . . . preached from house to house . . . the hope is entertained that the love of the Church may yet revive in the parish." That fond hope was finally realized when the church was rebuilt in 1848 and re-dedicated as Grace Episcopal Church. Although T-shaped prior to the fire, only the central portion was rebuilt giving it the present-day appearance as shown in the sketch that heads this chapter. The marl walls were repaired, a new roof built, and a belfry has since been added.

No untoward incidents marred the even tenor of worship until war again swept the Peninsula, and blue-coated troops from the North occupied the town. Diagonally across the square from the church was the Courthouse which, this time, was selected as arsenal and powder magazine. For a while it seemed that the church would fare better in the Civil War than during the Revolution. True, her belfry was converted into a lookout and her interior was utilized as a hospital, but no serious damage was done to the building.

Then came an explosion that rocked the whole town. The Courthouse had blown up with its walls packed with gunpowder. The whole northwest end of town was destroyed and the church was again damaged. There is a tale that the original bell bearing the inscription "County of York, 1725" was blown from the belfry by this explosion and badly cracked. The crack was repaired, and the bell may still be seen in regular use tolling the faithful to services. Grace Episcopal Church continues to serve York-Hampton Parish in the Protestant Episcopal Diocese of southern Virginia.

Among the graves of the churchyard six generations of the Nelsons are represented, including that of "Scotch Tom" Nelson, the founder of the family in York County, and that of his illustrious grandson, General Thomas Nelson, Jr.

GENERAL THOMAS NELSON, JR.
PATRIOT, SOLDIER, CHRISTIAN GENTLEMAN,
BORN DECEMBER 12, 1738; DIED JANUARY 2, 1789,
MOVER OF THE RESOLUTION OF MAY 16, 1776, IN THE VIRGINIA
CONVENTION INSTRUCTING HER DELEGATES IN CONGRESS TO
MOVE THAT BODY TO DECLARE THE COLONIES FREE AND
INDEPENDENT STATE; SIGNER OF THE DECLARATION
OF INDEPENDENCE; WAR GOVERNOR OF VIRGINIA;
COMMANDER OF THE VIRGINIA FORCES.
"He Gave All for Liberty!"

The Thomas Sessions House

A TALE usually connected with Colonial houses in Virginia is that the brick "were brought over from England." In almost every case there is no basis for this assertion. Large quantities of stone and the hard burned "Dutch pavers," as well as square hearth and paving tile and the colorful Delft fireplace facing-tile were imported, but building brick seldom, if ever, found its way to the Colony.

The clay of Virginia has always been perfect for burning, and the Indians fashioned their earthenware pottery from it centuries before the white man came to these shores. When he did come, he brought brickmakers along in the first company to land at Jamestown with Captain John Smith in 1607.

The entire Tidewater country is covered with clay, as anyone who has attempted to drive over unsurfaced country roads during the rainy summer season or winter snows will well remember, and bricks have been made all over the state from clay immediately at hand. The usual custom, to avoid hauling, was to set up a kiln directly on or close by the building site and burn the brick "on the job." Remains of these early brick kilns are sometimes still encountered; a portion of the kiln used to burn brick for the main building of William and Mary College, built in

1695, was found on the college grounds during the restoration work of 1929. The great storm of 1933, washing away a portion of the river bank above Yorktown, revealed the remains of another ancient kiln.

The construction of the brick kiln and burning of the brick were very simple operations. A "press" or wood bin, about four feet square and five feet high, was set up and filled with clay. Through the center of the press stood an upright pole worked into a worm-screw shape at the bottom. A long, horizontal boom engaged the top of the pole at one end; its free end was drawn around in a circle by mules or oxen, thus rotating the worm-screw which compressed the clay, broke up the lumps, and forced it to the bottom of the press where it was fed out through a hole to be placed in wood forms or molds. These wood forms shaped the clay to the desired brick proportions and were always considerably larger than the actual finished brick size because of the shrinkage that took place in the clay when it was burned.

After molding in the forms to the proper shape and approximate size, the soft clay units thus achieved were spread out in the sun to dry out and harden for a few days. It was during this drying process that many of the old brick received the impressions of deer, wild boar, turkey, and small game footprints so often seen in the old brickwork. At this stage, too, the maker often scratched his initials or those of the prospective builder and the date into the soft clay.

Having been sufficiently sun-hardened, the clay units were next built into a kiln which was nothing but a series of small tunnels, or "eyes," formed by the units themselves, about two feet wide and high and about ten or fifteen feet long, depending upon the number of brick to be burned. The average kiln would burn about thirty thousand brick at a time. The clay units were placed about half an inch apart and stacked to a height of ten or twelve feet. Wood fires of oak or hickory were then lighted in the eyes and kept burning for several days. The fire was then allowed to burn out, and the clay units, now baked or "burned" into brick, given time to cool until they were ready for building purposes.

The brick ends or "headers" immediately next to the flame of the fire received the most intense heat. The direct flame sweated out and "glazed" the salts and minerals (which formed part of the clay composition) along the exposed face of the brick, giving them a colored, shiny surface ranging from light grays to greens and blacks, depending upon the natural mineral content of the clay, which varied in different localities.

These glazed headers were very much prized in Colonial work and may be seen worked into patterns of Flemish bond and fanciful rake or gable patterns in almost every brick house of any pretention in Tidewater. In some cases the chimney bricks were laid up in diaper patterns or panels of glazed headers.

Naturally, the brick at the top and sides of the kiln did not receive the same degree of heat as those closer to the fire and consequently did not receive as deep a color as the closer brick. This variation in color from deep red-oranges to faded salmon is what lends old brickwork its greatest charm and is so hard to duplicate in modern brick that is burned at a uniform high temperature to a sameness of color.

Another element of colonial brickwork that gave it character and beauty was the mortar, composed of oyster shell and coarse sand. Cement was never used in early brickwork in Yorktown; but a lime was made by burning, pulverizing, and slaking oyster shells. The lime paste thus realized was then mixed with white or yellow sand, and bricks laid up in oyster shell lime mortar usually had wide half-inch joints. The joints exposed on the face were, as a rule, incised or "struck" with a tool or the trowel point to give an interesting shadow line along the joints. The variation in the brick sizes was taken up in the mortar joints, and the struck line also helped to preserve an appearance of regularity.

Molded brick were very common in Colonial times and were formed in specially shaped molds, then burned the same as ordinary brick. They were used for watertables, belt courses, chimney caps, doorways, etc.

To gain another effect with brick, the corners of buildings, jambs, and brick arches of doors and windows, flat belt courses, and brick panels were often "rubbed," the surface of the brick face being scraped off with an abrasive, giving it a lighter or more intense shade than the field brick. These rubbed brick provided a pleasant contrast or frame for the building corners and openings. Jack, or flat, arches of brick were always "gauged" in later Colonial work. That is, the bricks were ground or shaped so that the vertical joints radiated from a common center like the spokes of a wheel.

The middle eighteenth century houses of Virginia employed several or all of these brick variations. A beveled or molded brick water-table course occurred at the line of the first floor, below which the basement or foundation walls were invariably laid in English bond, while above the watertable, equally invariably, Flemish bond prevailed.

The seventeenth century structures were considerably simpler. The watertable was also employed, but usually occurred only on the eave or long sides of the buildings, and Flemish bond was used both above and below the watertable. In this earlier work jack-arches were seldom used; segmental or row-lock arches of headers laid along the line of a shallow arc were being used instead.

The windows of the earlier buildings were usually much smaller than their Georgian successors and in many cases were fenestrated with leaded sash in diagonal or lozenge designs, set in metal frames. These old leaded sash have disappeared from Tidewater houses, but excavations on Jamestown Island have discovered several examples of the metal frames and fragments of the lead combing.

One of the best examples of the seventeenth century brick houses in York County is the Sessions House of Yorktown. It occupies Lot No. 56 which was first sold by the Town Trustees to Thomas Sessions on March 22, 1692. The first reference to a house being on the lot is made in a 1699 description of the lot next door, No. 57, which refers to the house on Lot No. 56 in relation to the common boundary between the properties. However, Sessions must have built upon the lot during his first year of ownership to retain title, so the reader may select either 1692 or 1693 as the building date. We prefer the earlier year, and cheerfully proclaim that the grand old house now occupying Lot No. 56 was built by Tom Sessions in 1692.

Sessions and his wife, Hester, owned the property for nine years, conveying title in 1701 to Robert Snead, from whom it passed through many and diverse ownerships.

The Sessions House is directly across Nelson Street from the Nelson House, and these two venerable monuments provide a fitting gateway to the most charming and delightful little lane imaginable. Nelson Street has, fortunately, never been blessed with paved surface or sidewalks, and it wanders back from Main Street for less than a full block. In that short, tree-shaded distance it travels miles from the busy highway, and a quality of peace and quiet prevails along its brief, flower-lined walks.

The flowered walks of Nelson Street are echoed in the grounds of the Sessions House with its box-bordered garden and the ivy-hung brick walls of the building. Built six years before the County seat was moved to Yorktown, it is the oldest house in town. Together with the Grace Episcopal Church and the old Lee House at Kiskiack, it completes the triumverate of the last seventeenth century structures still standing in York County.

In spite of its great age, the structure remains in excellent preservation, its massive brick walls and chimneys maintaining an appearance of great structural strength. The building has settled and adjusted itself to the most comfortable position on its site until it has attained that look of imperishable antiquity that graces certain ancient structures of a day far removed from our own — a look which seems to guarantee that, though fire and war shall reduce all else of Yorktown to rubble and ashes, the Sessions House shall remain.

In plan the first floor has the typical large central hall that is found in so many homes of the seventeenth and eighteenth centuries. Large rooms open off either side of the hall, at the rear of which a quaintly fashioned archway leads to the rear staircase serving the second floor. Much of the original interior woodwork remains although all of the mantels are gone.

The interior doors are of the conventional Colonial six-panel type to be found from Charleston to Boston, and in the Sessions House they are engaged to the door jambs by the equally typical wrought-iron H and L hinges, known, by some whimsy throughout this section, as "Holy Lord hinges." If there is a larger single door opening in all of Virginia than the front entrance to the Sessions House, many years of inquisitively peering at Colonial architecture throughout the State has not revealed it to us. The door itself measures forty-three inches in width and is handsomely paneled in a rather unusual arrangement of eight panels.

The eighteen-light windows of the first floor are large and well spaced, and above them occur the dormers inevitably found on gabled or gambreled roofs of the period. The roof, like that of the Swan Tavern, has curbed or snubbed gable-ends, hipped from a point half

67

1692
Hall Arch,
The Sessions House
Yorktown, Virginia.

way up the height of the gable. This method of roof construction shortened the otherwise long line of the ridge and gave a much more attractive appearance to the building, carrying the general outline of the roof back down to the ground and tying the composition in a manner much more satisfying than could be achieved by employing the straight and unrelieved gable peak. The dormer roofs are likewise snubbed rather than gabled.

The porches, both front and rear, are later additions to the original building. Seventeenth century architecture of Virginia closely patterned itself after that of the same period in England, where the weather did not generally permit for "porch settin'." The heat of Virginia summers and the long, lazy summer afternoons soon evolved this commendable practice; and porches (with mint patches planted conveniently at hand) sprouted throughout the Colony like mushrooms, not only as part of new houses but also as additions to old ones.

From Main Street the Sessions House presents a most engaging picture. With its ivy-hung, time-mellowed brick walls framed by the green of shrubbery and a back drop of large trees, it is elevated enough above the street level both to command and receive an excellent view. It has long been recognized as one of the most interesting and outstanding examples of early architecture in the Dominion.

The history of the house is not as interesting as its architecture. It was bought in 1766 by Dr. Matthew Pope who had been personal physician to the Royal Governor in Williamsburg. The good doctor's sympathies were, nevertheless, with the revolting colonists; and during the Revolution he twice served as Mayor of Yorktown.

The Sessions House rear wall bears no scars from either the Siege of 1781 or that of 1862. At the conclusion of the latter the house served as headquarters for General Negley of McClellan's staff during the Federal occupation of the town.

In 1901 the property was purchased by Conway H. Sheild, a Virginia lawyer, and has ever since remained in the family and become familiarly known as the Sheild House. Upon his retirement Judge Conway H. Sheild, Jr., who had been born in the house, made it his home until his death in 1970. His son, Conway H. Sheild III, following in the profession of his father and grandfather is a practicing attorney in Newport News. Many famous personages, including five presidents of the United States, have been among the visitors who have been attracted to this most singular old landmark, because of its antiquity, architecture, and location in the historic village.

The Archer Cottage

A VIEW of Yorktown from the river sketched by John Gauntlett of
H.M.S. *Norwich* in 1755 shows no less than forty-six buildings
along the waterfront covering the strip of five acres between the town
site and the river originally excluded from the Smith survey of 1691
as "a common shore of no value." As already noted in the Yorktown
chapter, this faulty appraisal was soon remedied; and a number of
storehouses, grogshops, dwellings, wharves, ferry landings, and other
waterfront facilities crowded the shore, some in fact having been
erected before the town lots were built upon.

The buildings of the town proper were by no means all dwellings,
a goodly number being retail stores, artisans' shops, inns, taverns, and
ordinaries, which were the lesser, in-between hostelries universally
called "ornaries." The establishment of any industry that would com-
pete with English manufacturers was not only discouraged but pro-
hibited, except for such minor activities as shoemakers, gunsmiths,
tailors, blacksmiths, etc. One such entrepreneur who seemed to have
evaded this restriction was a potter who maintained his kilns and plant
on Lot 51. Archaeological excavations conducted in 1970 clearly revealed the tunnel "eyes" of the kiln lined with header brick deeply

70

glazed by the firing that baked and glazed the molded clay bowls, mugs, and plates. Among the shards and fragments of the potter's products discovered at this site was a plate bearing the incised date "1720" indicating the potter was active at that time. In the Governor's annual reports, perhaps to minimize the conflict of this business with the prohibitive edict against manufacture, the individual concerned was described as "the poor potter of Yorktown."

Abraham Archer established himself in Yorktown as a merchant in 1729. Upon his death he left his business and properties to his son, Thomas, who in turn left several buildings "under the hill" to his sons, Abraham and Thomas, Jr. Among these buildings was the Archer Cottage, probably built either by their father or grandfather in the first half of the eighteenth century. It was apparently one of the two Archer sons referred to in Governor Nelson's letter of September 3, 1781, during the Siege, to Lord Cornwallis:

My Lord,

From the assurance given me in a letter I received from you of Aug. 5 — that all such Persons, as I described Messrs. Archer and Ryall to be, were ordered to be released, I rested satisfied those Gentlemen had obtained their Liberty. But I am just informed that they are still in Confinement on Board one of your Lordship's Prison Ships; which from your letter I must suppose to be a Circumstance with which you are not acquainted. I am therefore again to desire your Attention to these Gentlemen, & assure myself that you will order them to be released.

The Archer referred to could very well have been Abraham who became Naval Officer at Yorktown in 1782 as well as a County Magistrate.

The disastrous fire of 1814 wiped out the entire section of "Yorke Towne below the Hill," and although many of the structures were subsequently rebuilt, only one remains today, the Archer Cottage, a simple story-and-a-half frame structure rebuilt over the old stone foundation of the original building. The fire had left nothing standing but the stone masonry cellar walls and the exterior brick chimney, both of which attest to the early date of the first construction.

The masonry of the cellar walls is a combination of native marl stone and random ballast stones salvaged from the beach and laid up in rubble fashion without any attempt at regular coursing or jointing. The custom of jettisoning ballast stones from incoming ships on the shore or in the harbor eventually befouled the docking areas, and laws were enacted prohibiting ship masters from dumping ballast under penalty of fine.

The existing chimney of the Archer Cottage, laid up in English bond with alternating courses of headers and stretchers, is quite similar to the exterior chimneys of the Somerwell House from foundation to chimney cap. The Archer Cottage chimney is finished above the cap with an arched brick "bonnet" to prevent downdraft, not an unusual detail of the period.

While no record remains of the actual room arrangement of the original building, the reconstructed house built over the old foundations in the 1820's was no doubt quite similar to the first such structure, with a full undivided cellar and two rooms on each of the main and upper floors. Fenestration on both north and south elevations consisted of a center doorway flanked on either side by double-hung windows with unusual sash arrangements more often found in dormer sash; the lower sash being three lights high, the upper sash two. On each of these elevations, dormers with double-hung sash occur directly over the windows below, both upper and lower sash being two lights high. All windows are three lights wide except those flanking the chimney at the upper floor of the west elevation which are two lights wide. The east elevation has one window on each floor centered on the roof gable.

The wood framing studs of the building are covered on the exterior with drop siding or weatherboarding of the period; the interior walls are lathed and plastered.

The Archer Cottage was acquired and restored by the National Park Service as representative of a type of simple frame structure once occupying the waterfront.

Close by the Archer Cottage, hollowed out of the marl bank of the York River, is a cavern-like chamber which has existed from earliest times. Lord Cornwallis, forced to abandon the Nelson House where he had been headquartered during the Seige of 1781, met with his staff in a "grotto" below the river bank. As this cavern is the only such feature along the waterfront that would qualify as a "grotto", it has ever since been known as the "Cornwallis Cave."

The Thomas Pate House

THE year 1691 in Virginia was marked by the passage of an Act for Ports, intended to establish fifteen town sites along the rivers of the Tidewater to help unify the widely scattered tobacco plantations. In addition to providing ports of entry and export, these towns would centralize commerce and provide a means for "preventing frauds and better securing his Majesties customes." The provisions of the Act were published on June 3, 1691, and on the following July 24th a survey was started on the fifty acres of Benjamin Read's land which had been selected for the York County port town. Eighty-five half-acre lots were laid out and then put up for sale with a provision that the purchaser would forfeit title if he failed to build upon his property within one year.

The original purchaser of Lot 42 was John Seabourn, who apparently failed to place a structure upon the land. It was next granted by the Trustees to Thomas Pate in 1699, and he built a house upon it believed to be that still standing and now named for him. Then, on December 24th, 1703, Thomas Pate, the ferryman, and his wife, Elizabeth, deeded "my house & Lott," to Joan Lawson "in restitution and satisfaction of seven years service." Joan then sold Lot 42 to John Martin on September 24, 1705, and on January 18th, 1713, Martin sold it to Cole Digges. The sale to Digges was "together with ye housing thereon and appurtenances." The sale also included a storehouse owned by Martin located on the beach at the foot of Read Street.

Cole Digges was born about 1691, probably on the old "E.D. Plantation" at Bellfield. His mother, Susanne Cole Digges, was the daughter of William Cole, then Secretary of the Virginia Colony and his father, Dudley Digges, was the son of Governor Edward Digges and was the first Dudley Digges to be born in Virginia.

In 1708 Susanne Cole Digges died, leaving Lot 76 to her seventeen year old son, Cole. During the following years Cole became a prominent Yorktown merchant and, in 1719, was appointed to the Governor's Council. By 1729 his prosperous enterprises required additional warehouse space, and Cole was granted lease of an eighty foot square plot "below the bank at York Town adjoining to the place where his warehouse now stands for his convenience in building a commodious warehouse thereon . . . together with a wharf extending into the river." Finally, in 1731, Cole bought Lot 77 facing Main Street and on the inland side of his Lot 76. It was adjacent, also, to the "Great Valley" that gave access to "Yorktown below the hill," that colorful, glamorous section which was largely destroyed by fire in 1814.

Here were the wharves and warehouses, the ship chandlers and provisioners, taverns and rum-shops for seafaring men where "they cast the dice, swore brave oaths and drank merrily till late into the night." Here, during the days of the great tobacco fleets, the riverfront swarmed with as motley and picturesque a collection of characters as ever enlivened a Gilbert and Sullivan opera: ship captains and common sailors, naval officers from the British men-o'-war guarding the capes, planters and traders, slave dealers and their shackled wares, English adventurers and professional soldiers of every nationality, gamblers and pirates. Truly Yorktown-below-the-hill presented a picture splashed brightly with the gay colors of romance and high adventure.

Cole Digges departed this life in 1744; his third son, Dudley Digges, inherited the Yorktown Digges property. Dudley would become one of the more illustrious of the Digges. He kept the old house on Lot

42 until 1784 when he sold it to David Jameson. It was restored with meticulous care in 1925-26 by its owner at the time, Mrs. Carroll Paul of Michigan, in the form which it has today.

Yorktown-below-the-hill is no more, but the Thomas Pate House on top of the hill remains, not only as a reminder of days forgotten but as an example of all that was fine and most lasting in Colonial domestic architecture. A "heap of living" has made this little house a home for more than two and a half centuries, and its outward charm is such that many travelers driving by have exclaimed, "That is exactly the sort of house we have always wanted."

It is a low-eaved, snug little gabled cottage with white-washed brick walls all scrambled over with ivy. Minor alterations on the interior concede to modern comfort, but the original lines and mass of the building remain, preserving the neat and homely qualities of quiet dignity.

The roof cants back at the customary angled slope from which few Colonial roofs deviate; its angle is something less than a true forty-five degree pitch. One of the pleasantries of viewing a street of old houses, such as may be seen in Williamsburg, is the consistent manner in which all of the roofs parallel one another in slope.

The Pate House looks its best in winter with smoke curling from the chimneys and its lime white walls blending naturally into the snow-banked ground.

The Pate House
& Custom House,
Yorktown, Virginia.

The Old Custom House
Yorktown, Va.
1721

The Custom House

SHIP captains departing from or newly arriving in the Colony anchored their vessels in the York River and came ashore to climb the hill toward Main Street and the solid little two-story brick building in the center of town on Lot 43. Here they mingled with fellow skippers, learned the latest maritime news or the current tobacco prices, cleared their cargoes, registered their goods, attended to their marine insurance, paid the appointed Crown tax and tithes, obtained their sailing papers and, in general, conducted the usual shore business of their professions.

The little brick structure, although now known as the Custom House, was never a public building but was actually the private storehouse of one of Yorktown's leading merchants in the hey-day of the early eighteenth century tobacco trade. During that period Yorktown was the Virignia port of entry for all of the Northern cities, and ships and goods bound from Virginia for Philadelphia, New York, Boston, or England were forced to clear through the Yorktown Custom House. From its priority as one of the first controlled points of commerce and shipping in this country, it has been called the "Cradle of the American Tariff System."

Lot 43 originally had been bought from the Crown Trustees in 1691 by Captain Daniel Taylor who forfeited title due to failure to build thereon within the first year.

The second purchaser, in 1706, was George Burton, who must have erected some sort of structure as he still retained title upon his death when the property was left to his daughter, Ann. On January 11, 1721, Ann and her husband, Christopher Haynes, sold the lot to Richard Ambler. It is believed that Ambler replaced whatever improvements the Haynes may have had on the site with his own two story frame dwelling and the two story brick storehouse built in 1721. Lots 44 and 45 were acquired by him in 1726 for stables and a garden.

The Ambler dwelling was described as "a very commodious one, with four rooms above and four below." The other buildings on the property were "the large brick storehouse, kitchen, stables, washhouse and a well cultivated garden." During December of 1863 the dwelling was destroyed by the fire that spread from an explosion of gunpowder in the old Courthouse, but the storehouse, now known as the Custom House, exists today just as Richard Ambler built it.

The pleasant design and sturdy construction of this building is comparable to many other Colonial structures in Tidewater. Its thick brick walls are laid up in a careful pattern of Flemish bond with a checkered field of glazed headers broken at mid-height by a shallow, projecting brick belt-course. A neat cornice of graceful molding and wood modillions lends elegant embellishment to the eaves. At the corners the roof is framed with hips that pitch away to the ridge at a pleasing angle, providing a most happily proportioned crown for the mass of the building.

Fenestration of both stories is provided by large, eighteen-light windows with heavy shutters, while access to the interior is gained through handsome paneled doors of the period.

The pine woodwork of the interior has been left unpainted and in its natural color, a practice not uncommon during the early eighteenth century. In fact, as late as 1781 Robert Carter of Nomini Hall noted, "Wood artificers stain and polish wood with aqua-fortis and Linseed Oil mixt together — with this mixture they rub their work — afterwards rub it again with Linseed Oil only."

Richard Ambler, a successful merchant, occupied the office of

Collector of Ports during one of the most colorful and active periods in the history of Virginia. Alexander Spotswood was the Royal Governor, and under him the Knights of the Golden Horseshoe had established a new frontier beyond the Blue Ridge. The rapid growth of the tobacco trade and subsequent growth of the Colony caused a steady increase in shipping. The wharves of Yorktown witnessed a never ending pageant of ships loading and unloading; the goings and comings of sailors, merchants, inspectors, travelers, adventurers, planters, slaves, and bond-servants; in short, all of the color and excitement that made up a busy port.

As business prospered, Ambler added other properties in the town to his holdings, including a patent for a parcel of land along the waterfront on which he built a second storehouse and wharf in 1728.

Ships cargoes did not consist of merchandise and goods alone. The slave trade flourished, and slave ships often made Yorktown their home port where their human cargoes might be sold from the block at the Courthouse. Indentured servants also found ready sale throughout the Colony; and they were imported literally by the shipload, as witness the following *Gazette* advertisement:

> JUST ARRIVED. The Justitia, Captain Kidd, with about one hundred and thirty healthy servants, consisting of men, women, boys; among whom are many tradesmen, such as Carpenters and Joiners, Bricklayers, Plasterers, Shoemakers, Barbers, Hairdressers, Weavers, Cutters, Currieres, Bakers, Tanners, Tailors, Staymakers, Blacksmith, Printer, Miller, Stocking Weaver, Schoolmaster, Hatters, Silk Dyer and others. There are also many farmers, country laborers, Gentlemen's Servants, etc., etc. The sale will commence . . . on Wednesday, the 22nd instant, and be continued 'till all are sold. A reasonable credit will be allowed, the Purchasers giving bond with approved security to
>
> THOMAS MOORE.

At the Custom House, seafarers learned which ships had cleared port and gone on down to Lynnhaven Bay where the fleet for England was made up. No ship dared leave sight of land singly, because the Carolina capes swarmed with pirate craft ever on the alert for unguarded merchantmen. In the Chesapeake lay English men-of-war whose duty was to convoy the merchant fleet twenty-five or thirty leagues off the coast until there was no further danger from attack. Although the pirates roamed the coast and sometimes ran into bays and harbors to make their capture, they seldom ventured into the open ocean in search of their prey.

According to a report of 1717, there were fifteen hundred pirates on the Atlantic coast; but the manner in which this interesting census was arrived at is rather obscure. Of this era the outlaw of the sea best known to Virginia and the Tidewater was Blackbeard, the Pirate. Born in Bristol, England, as Robert Drummond, Blackbeard seems to have traveled under several aliases and spent most of his life afloat engaged in piracy. His soubriquet was applied due to the heavy black whiskers which he affected, but in his piratical exploits he was known by name throughout the Carolinas and Virginia as Robert Teach. In the official report of his last foray, he is called Tach; and on the court records that note his myriad depredations and final apprehension, he is inscribed as Edward Thatch. But as he has come down through history as Blackbeard, we will dispense with the variant nomenclature.

Legends of Blackbeard abound throughout the Tidewater. In spite of the known man-of-war patrol of Lynnhaven Bay in Colonial times, two shore points, Pirate's Fort and Blackbeard's Hill, are credited with having been lookout stations from which vantage this dauntless miscreant observed the movements of the merchant fleet in the bay. Rumor also has it that Blackbeard's treasure lies buried near Stratford Hall on the Potomac, and ominous night noises in various parts of the Tidewater country are still called "Blackbeard's guns."

To this *picaresque* fellow was attributed the somewhat questionable accomplishment of being able to whack off a head with a single blow of his broadsword. Another alleged curious and awesome habit was the practice of dipping his long black whiskers in some phosphorescent liquid that caused them to give forth a singularly infernal glow, a spectacle he no doubt found highly effective for terrifying the victims of his night attacks.

In 1718 Blackbeard had so terrorized the shipping of the Colony that the Governor and Council proposed that a reward of £100 be offered for his capture and £10 for each member of his crew. Governor Spotswood had tried for three years to convince the Admiralty that additional guardships were necessary in the Chesapeake to convoy the merchant ships, but his efforts met with surprisingly little response. So helpless did the authorities appear before the pirate menace that, on two occasions, the government in England found it necessary to grant a general amnesty to all pirates surrendering before a given date.

From one of these pardoned bucaneers, William Howard, a former quartermaster who had sailed with Blackbeard, Spotswood learned the pirate's place of refuge in an inlet of the Carolina coast. The outlaw was thought to have bought the connivance of Charles Eden, Governor of North Carolina, and it was even said that the Carolina governor had attended the marriage of Blackbeard to his fourteenth wife.

Without waiting for approval of King's Council or Assembly, Spotswood fitted out two sloops at his own expense, manned them with fifty-five men under Lieutenant Maynard, and sent them to seek out the pirate Blackbeard in his Carolina hiding place. This expedition found its quarry:

> . . . at Ouacock Inlett on the 22nd of last month (June 1718). He was on board a sloop wch. carryed 8 guns and very well fitted for fight. As soon as he perceived the King's men intended to board him, he took up a bowl of liquor and calling out to the Officers of the other sloops, drank Damnation to anyone that should give or ask quarter, and then discharged his great guns loaded with partridge shott, wch. killed and wounded twenty of the King's men . . . nor did any of his men yield while they were in a condition to fight. Tach (Blackbeard) with nine of his crew were killed, and three white men and six negros were taken alive but all much wounded. The loss of the King's men is very considerable for the number, there being ten killed in action, and four and twenty wounded of whom one is since dead of his wounds.

Blackbeard's severed head was suspended from the bowsprit on the homeward trip, and the three white men and six negroes taken alive were brought back to Williamsburg where, after trial, they were hanged along a stretch of Capitol Landing Road still known as Gallows Row.

The Governor of Maryland and several North Carolina skippers addressed grateful letters to Spotswood for the successful destruction of Blackbeard and his crew, but the Governor of North Carolina took considerable umbrage at armed intervention in Carolina waters by

Virginia vessels, claiming that the attack upon the pirates had been made without the authorization of the Carolina government. To this exposition of sheer ingratitude, Spotswood made fitting retort.

The overthrow of Blackbeard did not end the pirate activities, however. They continued to the end of Spotswood's administration, but the affair did rid the Carolina capes of one of the most vicious and heartless scourges of the sea.

The Governor of Virginia would sometimes go out on the bay to see the merchant fleet safely under sail. A "fleet" frequently numbered fifty vessels or more and on at least one occasion, as many as one hundred and forty ships sailed out of the Capes convoyed by four men-of-war.

All manners pertaining to the fleet were known to Richard Ambler. He knew their cargoes and destinations, their captains and owners with whom he no doubt traded gossip of the Colony for tidings from abroad. It was probably from Ambler at the Custom House, for instance, that mariners first learned of Governor Alexander Spotswood's scandalous squandering away of the public funds on his "palace" in Williamsburg.

Richard Ambler married Elizabeth, daughter of Edward Jacquelin, in 1739, the same year in which the elder Jacquelin died leaving to his new son-in-law the estate at Jamestown. The ruined walls of this once stately mansion may still be seen on Jamestown Island and are now known as the remains of the Jacquelin-Ambler House.

Upon his death in 1766, Richard Ambler left his Yorktown properties, including the waterfront storehouse to his son, Edward; the land at Jamestown went to son John and the balance of his estate, which included several acres outside of Yorktown, was divided between sons John and Jacquelin. Their son, Jacquelin, had been given his mother's maiden surname; hence, the unusual first name.

John Ambler served in the Assembly as Representative from Jamestown until his death in the same year as his father's, 1766, whereupon he was succeeded in this post by his brother, Edward, who outlived him only a year, dying in 1767.

Son Jacquelin, however, decided to follow his father's successful mercantile career and exchanged his holdings with brother Edward, thereby coming into possession of both dwelling and storehouses in

Yorktown. Like his father before him, Jacquelin also served as Collector of Ports and, in addition, took an active part in the political affairs of the Colony as Sheriff of York County. He was made a member of the Council in 1780 and, upon formation of the State of Virginia, served as Treasurer until his death in 1798.

At the outbreak of the Revolution, Jacquelin Ambler vacated his Yorktown property which was taken over as barracks by the Virginia Militia. The troops so damaged the house, fences, outhouses, and garden "as to put it out of his power to make it a comfortable residence for his family" that he petitioned the House of Delegates in 1776 to take it over upon payment to him of "a reasonable sum"; a petition that was denied. Apparently the house itself was not too badly damaged because Jacquelin sold it in 1778 to Thomas Wyld, Jr., who operated an ordinary in the dwelling until forced out by the British during the Siege of 1781.

The Revolution and Siege hastened the decline of Yorktown's commercial activities. One of the Brady Civil War photographs, showing the Custom House, is captioned "Head-quarters of General Magruder at Yorktown." The picture includes the ruins of the Ambler House immediately west of the Custom House.

Spared by the sieges of two wars and the great conflagration of 1814, the Custom House has seen its contemporary neighboring buildings go down before the ravages of battle, fire, and time until an ignominious demise from old age and lack of repair seemed its own fate.

Happily, the building has been spared this inglorious ending. The Comte de Grasse Chapter of the Daughters of the American Revolution, recognizing and appreciating the historic worth of the grand old landmark, purchased the property for their chapter house in 1924. With funds donated by one of the chapter members, Mrs. Arthur Kelly Evans of Hot Springs, Virginia, restoration was brought about in 1929; and through the good offices of the Comte de Grasse Chapter, the Custom House will be perpetually preserved as one of the first and oldest structures of its kind in this country.

During the Sesquicentennial Celebration of October 16-19, 1931, four memorials were dedicated at the Custom House: THE DE GALLATIN TABLET in honor of Baron Gaspard de Gallatin, presented by Major William E. Besse, of Torrington, Conn., to the Daughters of the

American Revolution of Virginia, unveiled October 16; THE DE GRASSE TABLET in honor of Comte de Grasse, presented by the National Society, Sons of the American Revolution, unveiled October 17; THE GOOCH TABLET in honor of Major William Gooch, presented by Mrs. J. McNeely, of Lincolnton, N.C., unveiled October 18; and THE NELSON TABLET in honor of Governor Thomas Nelson, Jr., presented by the Daughters of the American Revolution, unveiled October 18.

The Dudley Digges House

SHOULD a commission ever be appointed to select one specific house of the Colonial period that would portray in its plans, details and proportions the typical house of Tidewater Virginia, perhaps no better choice could be made than the Dudley Digges House in Yorktown.

Its large, full-depth central hall, similar to many found in houses large and small throughout the Colony; the general arrangement with two rooms opening off each side of the hall; the rear open-string staircase with its gracefully turned balusters and ornamented facings; the corner fireplaces grouped to make only two chimneys necessary; are all details of the plan and disposition of rooms and major appointments of the type of house most generally built throughout the Old Dominion.

Many more sumptuous dwellings were built and the Dudley Digges House cannot be compared with the great manor houses of the mighty plantations. However, these were in their day, as they are now, outstanding architectural examples and not typical of the thousands of more humble dwellings that housed the greater number of the colonists.

It might be said that because so many examples of brick architecture remain in Virginia the truly typical structure should be of brick. No one can deny the numbers of brick houses extant, but during the eighteenth century the frame dwellings far outnumbered their brick neighbors. Destruction by time and fire has, naturally, removed more of the wood buildings than the more enduring brick dwellings.

The outstanding characteristic of the Tidewater dwelling was simplicity — a simplicity not derived by severity of line and absence of ornament, but through a line and proportion of dignified repose with a judicious and restrained use of classical architectural forms. The simple dignity of the Dudley Digges House is most eye-arresting in its visual appeal. From any angle the building presents a pleasing picture, although there are no unusual details to lend the house a style or distinction that would differentiate it from its class. It is of the story-and-a-half type of construction with a full first story and a simple gable roof that makes necessary the employment of dormer windows to light the second floor. Large well-proportioned windows fenestrate the front or street elevation symetrically about the center entrance on the first floor and dormers occur over each opening below.

The use of certain combinations of molding, types and arrangements of panels, turnings and carvings was so universal as to be almost what today's architect calls "stock" details. The rounded or beaded edge was so widely employed that it is almost impossible to find a sharp corner throughout all Tidewater. This practice pertained even to the edging of weatherboarding, door and window jambs, all casework and was continued in the design of furniture. This house has a superabundance of beading on both the interior and exterior woodwork.

The most common cornice for both interior and exterior work was the three-member combination of crown, fascia, and bed-molding. In houses of its size the main exterior cornice was amplified with another band consisting of wood modillion blocks, and true to form, the Dudley Digges House employs this simple modillioned exterior cornice.

Perhaps the most interesting phase of the house is the parlor, paneled from floor to ceiling, with the panels broken by a molded chair rail. A delightfully naive arch treatment leads to the rear room. The paneling retains its original paint colors which were a rather alarming combination of lavenders, greens, and golds now so mellowed and softened by time as to barely suggest the vivid hues they must have originally presented.

Unlike most early structures on Main Street the house is set back from the front property line. The building occupies Lot 77 on land originally purchased in 1691 by David Stoner who forfeited title due to failure to build thereon. In 1706 Miles and Emanuel Wills acquired the property, retaining it until 1721. Archaeological excavations have uncovered brick foundations of an earlier structure at the front of the lot that may have been built by the Wills brothers and also may explain why the Dudley Digges House is set back from the street; the older building probably remained occupied until the later one was completed.

William Stark, the merchant, bought the property from the Wills brothers in 1721, retaining title until 1731 when he sold it to Cole Digges, grandson of Governor Edward Digges. Upon Cole's death in 1744 his yougest son, Dudley, inherited the father's Yorktown holdings that then included Lots 39, 42, 76, and 77. Being only sixteen at the time, Dudley continued his residence at the old Cole Digges House on Lot 42 in which he had been born.

Dudley married Martha Armistead in 1747, and they had two children, Cole and Patsy; Martha died at the latter's birth in 1757. Two years later he married Elizabeth Wormley, and they had five children, Elizabeth, Mary, Dudley, Jr., Lucy, and Judith.

In 1755 Dudley added Lot 79, adjacent to the east of Lot 77, to his property. Together with Lot 76, adjacent to the north, the three lots gave him a proper setting for his new home which he built about this time on Lot 77. A plat plan accompanying an insurance policy of 1796 shows the outline of the house with Lot 79 largely given over to a group of outbuildings identified as kitchen, granary, smokehouse, well, and stable.

By the middle of the eighteenth century the spirit of independence had so developed in the colonies that it colored not only the political thought of the colonists but affected their own attitudes of themselves. They no longer considered themselves as transplanted Englishmen, but as Virginians, Carolinians, Pennsylvanians, and Vermonters.

To England, unfortunately, they still remained Englishmen, subject to any restrictions which Parliament and the King felt inclined to impose.

The result of this conflict of interests and ideas was inevitable; and throughout the colonies, feelings seethed with such intensity that the

Revolution might easily have broken out at any time during the twenty years preceding 1775. In 1773 word had been received in Virginia that persons accused of treason in America were to be transported to England for trial. The Burgesses, meeting at Williamsburg, passed heated resolutions denouncing this proposed new policy and repeated them a year later when they learned that an Act of Parliament had sealed the harbor of Boston with an armed force of British regulars. Upon this action in the House of Burgesses, the Royal Governor, John Murray, Earl of Dunmore, immediately dissolved the Assembly.

Undaunted, the Burgesses reassembled the next day, May 27, 1774, in Raleigh Tavern at Williamsburg, and proceeded to draft the following proposal:

> . . . we . . . are . . . clearly of Opinion that an Attack, made on one of our Sister Colonies, to compel submission to arbitrary Taxes, is an Attack made on all British America, and threatens Ruin to the Rights of all, unless the united Wisdom of the whole be applied. And for this Purpose it is recommended to the Committee of Correspondence that they communicate with their several corresponding Committees, on the Expediency of appointing Deputies from the several Colonies of British America to meet in general Congress . . .

The Committees of Correspondence had been first suggested the previous year by a small group of the Virginia Burgesses who had proposed that a commission be appointed in Virginia to secure information concerning the actions of Great Britain, and to communicate with the other colonies in this regard. Action following these proposals brought about the forming of similar commissions in the other colonies, and during the ensuing year these Committees of Correspondence carried on a lively exchange of communications.

Yorktown and York County were represented in the "immortal eleven" of the Virginia Committee of Correspondence by Dudley Digges. His ten fellow conspirators were Peyton Randolph, Robert Nicholas, Richard Bland, Richard Henry Lee, Benjamin Harrison, Edmund Pendleton, Patrick Henry, Dabney Carr, Archibald Cary, and Thomas Jefferson—patriots all.

The proposals of the Virginia Committee led to the convening of the first Continental Congress in Philadelphia, held during September of 1774, and of the seven delegates selected to represent Virginia, six were members of the Committee of Correspondence and the seventh was George Washington. Six months later, on April 19, 1775, came the battle of Lexington in Massachusetts and the Revolution began.

Dudley Digges, a close friend of Patrick Henry, distinguished himself during the Revolution, and became one of the most respected and influential Virginians of his day. In addition to his service during the Revolution, he served as Burgess from York County for twenty-five years (1752-1776); Comptroller of Customs at Yorktown from 1770 to 1776; Member of the Virginia Council from 1776 to 1781; and Rector of William and Mary College from 1782 to 1784.

During the Siege of 1781 British officers presumably were quartered in the house until the bombardment of the Allies intensified. The Dudley Digges House was within their range and several cannon balls went through the building. Dudley moved his residence from Yorktown to Williamsburg after the Revolution. In 1787 he deeded the old Dudley Digges House in Yorktown to his daughter, Elizabeth, who had married Robert Nicholson. Dudley Digges died in 1790, at age 62.

In 1818 the house was owned and occupied by Major John R. West and his wife, Elizabeth, daughter of Governor Thomas Nelson. Major West was a descendant of Lieutenant Colonel John West, whose exploits have been treated in some detail in this book's chapter on Bellfield and who had, in fact, sold the Bellfield lands to Governor Edward Digges in 1650. Today the old Dudley Digges House is in excellent state of preservation, having been restored in 1960 by the National Park Service.

The Mungo Somerwell House

A BIRD'S-EYE VIEW of the Virginia Colony in the middle eighteenth century would have disclosed an antlike procession of
English travelers, that indefatigable tribe restlessly crawling around
the world like fruit flies around a wrinkled apple. They came, they
looked, they saw, and then scurried to the nearest *escritoire* to pen their
impressions and observations to their families and friends, to their
families' friends and to their friends' families; in fact, to anyone they
thought might sit still long enough to read what they had written. It
was the Golden Age of letter-writing when style and a flourish colored
the written word of even the humblest literate.

In these days of newspapers, radio, and television, when news is
spread instantly to the four corners of the world, it is difficult for us to
visualize the conditions of those earlier times when private correspondence was the main vehicle for carrying the news.

Fortunately for the research worker intent upon gathering information pertaining to the Colonial period, a wealth of such letters, accounts, and journals remains for our perusal; and it is from such a letter
published in 1764 in the *London Magazine* that we learn of one Eng-

lish traveler's impressions of Yorktown. "Yorktown," he wrote, "makes no inconsiderable figure. You perceive a great air of opulence amongst the inhabitants who have, some of them, built themselves houses equal in magnificence to many of our superb ones at St. James, as those of Mr. Lightfoot, Nelson etc. . . ." The Lightfoot House referred to by this chance traveler was the home of a successful merchant, Philip Lightfoot.

The first members of the Lightfoot family known to have settled in Virginia were the two brothers, John and Philip, who came from Northamptonshire, England, to Gloucester County around the middle of the seventeenth century. They were grandsons of Richard Lightfoot, Rector of Stoke Bruerne, and sons of John Lightfoot, Barrister-at-Law. John, the older brother, was appointed Auditor General of the Virginia Colony in 1670.

Philip served as Lieutenant Colonel of the Gloucester County Militia and in 1676 was appointed Surveyor General; in the same year, according to official reports, being "a great Looser and Sufferer both in Estate and person being both plundered and imprisoned by the Rebells"; the latter being the followers of Nathaniel Bacon, leader of Bacon's Rebellion. Philip subsequently moved to James City County where he served as Justice of the Peace and Collector for the Upper District of James River. He died in 1708 and lies buried at Sandy Point in what is now Charles City County.

Philip had two sons, Francis and Philip, Jr., and it was the latter, born in 1689, who built the Yorktown house referred to in the letter quoted above. Son Philip had established himself in York County as early as 1707, in which year he served as County Clerk, maintaining this appointment until 1733.

Setting up as a trader and merchant, Philip, Jr., acquired his first Yorktown property with the purchase of Lot 38 in 1709 and apparently built on the site as he continued to retain title thereto. As his successful mercantile career flourished, he added to his Yorktown holdings by purchasing Lot 16 in 1715; Lot 36 in 1716; Lots 7 and 13 in 1718; Lot 22 in 1724; Lot 17 in 1732; and Lot 11 in 1733. At the time of his death in 1748, besides his Yorktown lots, his estate included property in eight other counties.

Philip's success as a merchant was a matter of concern and distress to others with similar aspirations, it being recorded in a letter following his demise that, "Col. Philip Lightfoot is now dead, so that you can never have so fair a way open'd to you for establishing a store, as at the present time; his great riches while he continued in health deterred everybody from settling here, none being of ability to vie with him but Mr. Nelson, who always had an equal share of trade with him."

Philip built his first house on Lot 16; Lots 11 and 17 being soon added to accommodate stables, outbuildings and gardens. The second and largest of the Lightfoot houses, located between the Courthouse and the York River, was built high on the bluff overlooking his waterfront storehouse and wharf along the river known as "Colonel Lightfoot's Landing." It was a pretentious brick mansion erected on Lot 22 at or about the time he acquired the property in 1724. This house remained his Yorktown residence until his death in 1748, and was the "home of the successful merchant, Philip Lightfoot" mentioned in the *London Magazine* item above quoted.

In or about 1718 Philip married Mary Armistead Burwell, widow of James Burwell. Philip and Mary had four sons, William, Philip, John, and Armistead. All four, however, were deceased before their widowed mother who died in 1775. Upon her death the Yorktown house was left to her grandaughter, Mary, the only child of son Armistead and his wife, Anne Burwell. The grandaughter married Dr. John Taylor Griffin, and in 1777 the Griffins rented the house to Thomas Wyld, Jr., who advertised his use of the building as an ordinary that year, describing it as "the property of Dr. John Griffin, and formerly belonging to Mrs. Lightfoot."

Following the fire of 1814 which left the house undamaged, the ladies of the town were cared for "under the spacious and hospitable roof of Major Griffin's house." During Lafayette's visit to Yorktown in 1824, "Major Griffin's romantic house" served as host-house for the invited guests; the "Major" being Dr. Griffin's son, Thomas. These two references indicate that the house withstood the Siege of 1781 and may well have been the building described in an insurance policy taken out by Thomas Griffin in 1832.

The exact date of its destruction is indeterminate; but as it was adjacent to the Courthouse on Lot 24, it may have been destroyed by fire resulting from an explosion of gunpowder in the Courthouse during its occupancy by Union troops in 1863.

The famous old house of Philip Lightfoot is gone, but another of his properties, the brick building on Lot 36 at the northeast corner of Church and Main Streets, remains, although he was not the original owner or builder. Lot 36 was first bought in 1691 by William Digges, who forfeited title due to failure to build thereon. For eight years the lot then remained under trusteeship until, in 1699, it was taken up by Robert Leightonhouse, a teacher turned innkeeper. Robert's widow, Elizabeth, married the York River ferryman, Mungo Somerwell, and it is believed the existing brick structure was one of the "several buildings and improvements" erected on the lot by Somerwell.

In 1707, upon the death of Mungo, valid title was granted to Elizabeth who subsequently took as her third husband, Edward Powers. Elizabeth Powers died intestate and her sole heir, Joseph Mountfort, inherited her property in 1716, conveying the house and lot to Philip Lightfoot by deed in the same year.

Philip had apparently bought the property for an income investment, as at the time of his purchase the house was being operated as an ordinary by one Mary Smith. Upon his death in 1748 the house and lot were left to Philip's eldest son, William, who in turn left it to *his* son, Philip, the nephew of the successful merchant.

Lot 36, the westerly half of which contains the house, abuts Grace Episcopal Churchyard along its northerly property line, faces south on Main Street and occupies a key position in the plan of the town. Past its corner at the intersection of Main and Church Streets all the life of the town flowed. The elect of the upper town swept by in broadcloth and powdered wig on their way to the Courthouse. The Sabbath congregations turned at the corner on their Sunday morning promenades to and from Divine Service at the old Church; all the colorful traffic of coach, carriage, and saddle raised Main Street's summer dust or splashed its winter mud as it passed by the house.

Philip Lightfoot, the nephew, and his wife, Mary Walner, sold the property to John Moss of Richmond in 1783, the year that peace was finally gained by the Treaty of Paris. Thus various members of the Lightfoot family held title for sixty-seven years. During that time they saw Yorktown develop into a thriving commercial town. They lived through the terrible days of the Revolution and experienced the Siege of 1781. From their property they may have seen the sky glow with the flames of the burning British fleet. The bombardment of the French and Colonial forces may have fallen upon their ears as the crack of doom, and they probably saw many of their neighbors' houses destroyed by the cannonading. It is even possible that their building was struck, explaining many of the puzzling patches in the brick walls that show decided evidence of very early repair, perhaps made necessary by the passage of cannon balls.

John Moss of Richmond built a store on the eastern half of the lot and in 1798 deeded the store to another John Moss of Yorktown, while six years later the western half of the lot containing the house was conveyed to Peyton Southall.

The two halves of the lot were once more joined in 1812 when Southall's administrator obtained title to both properties. The lot was divided again by sale in 1885 and has remained so divided until recently. It was the western half of the lot occupied by the house and the remains of certain ancient outbuilding foundations that became the property of the United States Government through purchase in 1930.

During the Civil War a stable was moved behind and joined to the rear wing, and the structure was traditionally used as a hospital for the Federal troops. After the Civil War the entire structure was made into a hotel, and the stable addition was added to by a long, rambling, two-story frame structure of bedrooms with an additional full story added over the stable portion which was originally only one story.

The earliest insurance record available (1817) indicates the house in its original form was a T-shaped building of brick with wood shingle roof. It also shows a store building on the eastern half of the lot, probably the structure built by John Moss of Richmond around 1798. The outbuildings at the rear of the western half of the lot are also shown in their approximate locations and are noted as being a kitchen, stable, dairy, and smokehouse. Exploratory excavations conducted by the National Park Service in 1935 discovered ancient brick foundations at the sites shown on the insurance map as having been occupied by the stable, kitchen, and smokehouse; it is proposed to restore these structures together with the garden and other usual developments found on such estates. The dates of the erection of the outbuildings have not been determined, but in all probability they were much later than the main house itself. However, as listed in the insurance records, they were the

93

typical structures to be found in connection with dwellings of the style and period. If they were original to the early period of the house, they present certain puzzling phases that make their interpretation difficult in the light of restoration. For instance, the stable is noted in the insurance records as being sixteen feet square, but Peyton Southall, occupying the house from 1804 until 1812 had, according to his recorded inventory, three horses, two cows, a carriage, and a cart. It is difficult to see how he managed to keep them all in such a small stable.

In general appearance the exterior of the house is typical of many such brick homes of that locale and period. It is particularly similar to the old Glebe House of Gloucester County in both plan and construction details.

The walls are laid up in solid brick masonry patterned in Flemish bond above the beveled brick watertable that occurs at the line of the first floor, and in English bond below the watertable. The brickwork is further embellished by glazed headers of a dark greyish-green that contrast and at the same time blend with the dull orange-reds of the field brick. The chimneys are as well proportioned in their height, breaks, mass, and relation to the gable ends they grace as any throughout the Tidewater; and they serve separate fireplaces for each room of the first floor and all but one of the second floor.

The rambling modern frame wing in the rear of the original building was razed in 1935 when restoration began. From the maze of rooms and corridors of the old Yorktown Hotel the original brick building, phoenix-like, has been restored to its 1781 appearance. The restoration was completed by the National Park Service in 1937, and the house is used as a single-family residence by the Park.

Ye Swan Tavern, 1722
Yorktown, Virginia.

The Swan Tavern

FROM an early letter we are reminded how the Virginia colonists "lived freely, for it was a liberal time, and liberal fashions were in vogue, and it was not for a Virginian to be behind others in hospitality and liberality. There was one consolation if the Virginian involved himself like a fool, he suffered himself to be sold out like a gentleman. He knew nothing of the elaborate machinery of ingenious chicane. Accordingly he kept tavern and made barter of hospitality, a business the only disagreeable part of which was receiving money."

This genteel picture of the Colonial tavernkeeper is not completely borne out by other records which make no doubt of the reason many worthies kept a hostelry—because it was a profitable venture—and they did not suffer embarassment in finding it necessary to accept emolument in return for their hospitality.

The early taverns of the Colony varied all the way from rude log cabins in the Indian wilderness, wherein the entertainment consisted of "bacon, whiskey and Indian bread," to the more effete Gadsby's Tavern of Alexandria, the famous Raleigh of Williamsburg, and the Swan Tavern of Yorktown. The inns were usually tippling places where liquor was sold without providing food or lodging for travelers; the ordinaries provided mainly food, with some sleeping accommodations, while the taverns were the large hotels of the day.

Two factors which brought about the free and expansive manner of Virginia taverns were the standard of open-handed hospitality which radiated from the great plantations and extended into the normal life and conduct of the times, and the great distances between settlements.

Visiting was such a common and continuous custom that a large portion of the planters and their families were always enroute to or from the plantation of a friend or relative. There is a story of a newly married couple who, having agreed to spend a week or two of their honeymoon with each of a large circle of plantation friends, were over two years in returning to their own plantation.

At first there were so few towns and villages that every cabin, farm, and plantation was in effect a tavern and every settler a landlord. No charge was made for the entertainment of chance travelers whose visit was a pleasant break in the secluded life of farm and forest.

The first taverns were simple affairs of only one or two rooms with practically no conveniences. The fare was obtained locally—game from the woods and fish from the streams with corn, potatoes, and the common cereals from the nearby clearing. Taverns were favorably located along the most traveled roads and were the only means, in many cases, convenient for the accommodation of travelers and relief of horses.

As the roads of Colonial Virginia were poorly maintained and the main traffic followed the rivers, every point of embarkation provided rest for the weary traveler, the thirsty sailor, and the hungry wayfarer. Inns, ordinaries, and taverns almost automatically supplied this demand. Recalling that the majority of such travelers were of English birth and that the English inns and ale-houses were practically national institutions, it can be readily understood why the practice was repeated in the Colonies.

With the increase in travel, the general improvement of roads, and the advent of stage-wagons and coaches, these first primitive establishments were rapidly replaced with more or less comfortable taverns. Soon there were many such hostelries throughout Tidewater with "quaint signs, smiling bonifices and everything to match." The signs, besides bearing the name of the tavern and owner, announced to travelers that here might be found "entertainment for man and beast."

In the early days of the Colony reading was not as universal an accomplishment as it is today, and carved and painted signboards that would attract the eye and mark in the memory the site advertised were much in use. It was an old English custom reproduced in this country, and landlords vied with each other in the variety of designs and elegance of execution in their signboards.

Of all the hundreds of such signboards which must at one time have marked the many shops and taverns of Tidewater, none remain. In providing signs for the restored buildings of Williamsburg and Yorktown it has been necessary to copy either photographs or early prints of the originals or copy designs of existing New England and English examples.

The first ordinary on the York River preceded even the founding of Yorktown because on February 24, 1690, Robert Read was granted a license "to keep an ordinary at the place where the fferry now is kept upon the South side of the York River." In 1694 Thomas Pate, the ferryman, was also granted such a license. Pate, it will be recalled, is credited with building the Cole Digges House on Lot 42.

On August 24, 1692, Captain Thomas Mountfort was granted his license to keep an ordinary on Lot 37, the first such establishment within the town limits above the riverfront. Mountfort continued operation of this ordinary until his annual license was rejected in 1707.

Alexander Young, the original purchaser of Lots 60 and 61, was granted a license in 1697 to keep an ordinary "in Yorktown where hee now lives"; probably on one or the other of his two lots.

A number of early innkeepers of Yorktown had originally followed other professions; Robert Leightonhouse had been a teacher; Thomas Sessions a carpenter; Peter Gibson a gunsmith. The latter and his brother, Use, purchased Lots 58 and 62 from the original owner, Robert Harrison, in 1702, and set up an ordinary thereon.

At the sign of the Swan in Yorktown there flourished a tavern that remained one of Virginia's most famous "publick houses" for over one hundred and forty years. Situated directly across from the Courthouse, at the southeast corner of Main and Ballard Streets, the principal approach to the river, this tavern was most favorably located, drawing trade from the shipmasters, traders, and inspectors of the wharf, the sessions of the Court, and the merchants of the town. Being also on the stage route to Williamsburg, it was patronized by travelers the year round.

The land upon which the Swan Tavern was built was "That lot or half acre of Land scituate in York Towne there known by ye number 25 as by ye Plat on Record doth appear," and was first taken up from the Crown Trustees by "Charles Hansford, Gent. on November 24; 1691, and by him deserted." Having reverted to the Trustees, the lot remained in their hands for fourteen years until January 8, 1706, when "Daniel Taylor, Gent." came forward with the purchase price of 180 pounds of tobacco. Dan and his wife, Mary, sold their property to James Sclater the next year. Sclater and his wife, Mary, held on to the lot for nine years when it was conveyed to Benjamin Clifton in

1716. He in turn sold it on August 17, 1719, to "Scotch Tom" Nelson and Joseph Walker; and it was these individuals who, a year or two later, built upon the lot "a Tenement commonly called the Swan" which was "first opened as a House of Entertainment on the 18th of March, 1722," with Robert Wills as innkeeper almost twenty years before the Raleigh was opened in Williamsburg.

In 1742 William Nelson, eldest son of "Scotch Tom," bought out Walker's interest and, in 1761, conveyed the lot with the buildings "known by the name of the Swan Tavern" to his son, Thomas, who became General of the Virginia Militia during the Revolution and later third governor of the new state of Virginia.

Perhaps the best known host of the Swan was James Mitchell who was first granted a license in 1742 "for keeping an ordinary at the Swan in York Town." For the next thirty years Mitchell served as the "smiling Boniface" until his death in 1772. The tavern remained in the Nelson family until 1778 when it was sold for £1000 to Lawrence Gibbons who operated it for ten years. Lawrence Smith lived in and operated the Swan from 1788 until 1811, and the next year it was sold to our old friend, Preacher Scervant Jones.

The tavern building was a large story-and-a-half frame structure built above the sturdy brick walls of a full basement. The first floor contained four large rooms which opened off a wide central hall. The plan was repeated on the second floor. One of the rear front rooms was the taproom and, as was typical in most taverns of that time, was the most important and most frequented room in the establishment. Except for the roof and dormers being hipped, the Swan Tavern building is quite similar in size, construction, and fenestration to the Dudley Digges House on Lot 77.

Guests seeking accommodations must first apply to the barkeeper, who was generally also the host. This custom was no doubt designed to entice the wary guest into the taproom where he would be immediately prevailed upon to sample the wares of the bar, being at the same time cautioned by the host's motto which hung in plain view on the wall:

> "My liquor's good, my measures just,
> But, honest Sirs, I will not trust."

In spite of this blunt warning the host usually did trust, and the old ledgers of Swan Tavern show many debts accrued to guests' accounts for liquor and gambling.

Across the bar of the taproom were dispensed a great variety of drinks: whisky, peach brandy, French brandy, rum, Madeira wine, "cyder," ale, and metheglin, a favorite Virginia drink made of the long beans of the honey-locust. Of mixed drinks there were an infinite number. Summer brought its demand for rum swizzles, mint juleps, iced punches, arrack and sack. Winter provided the season for steaming toddies, hot rum drinks, and spiced wines.

The brick-walled basement held pipes of wines, casks of brandies, kegs of beer, and barrels of whisky. It was a boozy age, and if all of the eighteenth century rum bottles that have since been dug up at Yorktown were to be laid end to end they would reach from the once well-stocked cellars of the Swan Tavern to the taproom of old Raleigh Tavern in Williamsburg.

The daily menu was prepared with little difficulty at the Swan. Besides a choice of native venison, bear, wild turkey, and small game of all kinds, fresh from the kill or hung to the taste, there were fish of a dozen varieties, clams, oysters, crabs, and shrimp; the kitchen was always well-stocked with fresh vegetables from the tavern garden patch, and wild herbs, berries, nuts, and fruits were to be had for the gathering. Corn pone, hoe cake, and batter breads were standard items for every meal; on special festive occasions, culinary masterpieces were offered that for ingenuity and skill of cookery remained long in the memories of the partakers. The fare was heavy, but in those strenuous times a heavy fare was essential. In 1807 an English traveler wrote:

> It was the custom in all American Taverns, to have a sort of public table at which the inmates of the house and travelers dine together at a certain hour. At half-past seven . . . the bell rings, the dining room door is unlocked, a general rush commences and some activity as well as dexterity is essentially necessary to obtain a seat at the table. The breakfast consists of a profusion of fish, flesh and fowl, which is consumed with a rapidity truly extraordinary. At two o'clock the bell rings announcing the approach of dinner, the doors are thrown open and a repetition of breakfast succeeds. At six, tea, or what is here called supper, is announced and partaken of in the same manner. This is the last meal and usually affords the same fare as breakfast.

The sleeping rooms commonly contained from four to eight beds with mattresses, sheets, blankets, and quilts; but when travel on the road was heavy, it was no unusual occurrence for those unable to obtain beds to sleep on the floor of the public rooms. A ten o'clock "nearly all have gone to bed, or what they call 'turned in'."

Between supper and "turning in" the guests gathered in the tap-room or sat around the fire. The nightly conversation of the crowd assembled around the tavern hearth or crowding the bar was the equivalent of our modern radio. Here new ideas were discussed, political problems harangued, and affairs of the Colony in general were debated.

Lord Dunmore's Point Pleasant Campaign of October, 1774, had taken many militiamen of Virginia and Carolina across the mountains and into "Kaintuck." After discharge from this military service the soldiers carried home glowing tales of Kentucky, and the westward movement was in no small measure advanced through the gathering of many a tavern crowd about the fire to listen to the adventures of such a returned warrior.

Like most taverns of its day, the Swan also provided the setting for diversions, entertainments, and performances of all sorts: small theatricals, petty fakers, fortunetellers, freaks and dwarfs, amusing exhibitions of waxworks, and feats of dexterity and skill.

The tavern yard often served as the arena for wrestling matches and tests of strength, and the ever popular cock-fighting was usually conducted not too far from the convenience of a tavern bar. Most exciting of all public events were the drawings of lotteries, usually at the local tavern. This means of raising sums of money quickly amounted almost to a mania in the eighteenth century and was a favorite method used by schools, churches, and benevolent institutions of all kinds.

"Turkey shoots" and other shooting matches were sponsored by taverns in notices posted on the taproom walls, as were "bear-baiting" and "fox-chasing."

Tavernkeepers were required to post a bond of $150.00 with the York County Court for their tavernkeeper's license which, renewed annually, assured "good, wholesome and cleanly lodging and diet for Travellers and Stableage, fodder and provender or pasterage and provender as the season shall require for their horses." The license further avowed that tavernkeepers "shall not suffer or permit any unlawful gaming nor suffer any person to tipple and drink more than is necessary." Nobody, apparently, ever admitted to the indignity of being drunk in the eighteenth century; he merely drank more than was necessary.

The Swan Tavern was a place for assemblages of all kinds. One of its most famous owners, Robert Anderson, "a wealthy old gentleman well known throughout lower Virginia," who also ran a tavern in Williamsburg, advertised that the Swan offered "rooms for public meetings, courts martial, taking depositions, and such like assemblages" chargeable by the day. He further advised that as the Swan Tavern was "not intended to be a place of lazy, unprofitable resort, mere loungers are requested to keep away; and all who come only to idle their time at the fire in winter, or to gulp down ice water in the summer, will be charged, daily, twenty-five cents each."

Travelers and tavern patrons of the early days were often confronted with the problem of making change in payment for meals, lodging, and the keep of their horses. Small coins were so scarce and the use of the Spanish piastre and American dollar so common that the dollars were often cut into eight pieces or "bits" for circulation as small change, giving rise to the terms of "two-bits" and "four-bits" for a quarter and half-dollar respectively.

In the very early days of the Colony there was no Fourth Estate for the simple reason that the Governor, Sir William Berkeley, would not tolerate the printing of a newspaper in Virginia. In one of his reports to the Lord Commissioners of Foreign Plantations, Sir William gave vent to the following prayer:

> I thank God there are no free schools nor printing and I hope we shall not have them these hundred years; for learning has brought disobedience and heresy and sects into the world, and printing has divulged them. God keep us from both!

Divine Providence so willed it that, in spite of Sir William's lament, not much more than fifty years was to elapse before William Parks, the scrivener and printer, came to Williamsburg from Maryland and started the first newspaper in Virginia, which he called the *Virginia Gazette*. The first edition came out in 1736, and post-riders were employed to deliver the paper to subscribers in outlying districts. These riders also made regular trips for mail and brought back to their newspaper office news from correspondents at different points. They preceded the carrying of the mail by the stage lines, and nothing created more interest and excitement at the Swan Tavern than the arrival of the post-rider on his foam-flecked pony. Announcing his arrival with many a full, vigorous blast on the horn he carried, the post-rider was always assured of a waiting crowd to meet him.

Depositing his mail bag and papers at the tavern, he immediately became the center of a barrage of queries about the current news. He related what he had learned along his route, and each individual in the crowd repeated the news to his neighbor and family until everyone in the community had been informed of the news "both foreign and domestick."

We can only surmise what the temper of the people of Yorktown must have been when they heard the following account of the "Boston Massacre" as recorded in the *Virginia Gazette* of March 29, 1769, under the caption:

A SMALL RIOT REPORTED.

It is reported that a fray happened lately at Boston, between some of the inhabitants and some of the soldiers, and that the latter fired upon, and killed several of the former; whereupon a large number of the inhabitants rose, and (the report says) drove the soldiers out of the town, and the commissioners vanished, nobody knew where. We hope there is no truth in this report, but if there is a few days will clear it up.

The *Virginia Gazette,* together with London papers and the newspapers or "newsletters" of the larger Northern cities were taken by the Swan and made available to the public at large. It was the custom in early taverns to provide this service *gratis* and one purpose to which these tavern papers were put may be guessed from a notice posted over a taproom bar: "Gentlemen learning to spell are requested to use last week's newsletter."

Notices of events of civic or political interest were posted at the Courthouse, but outstanding events of a general or social nature were chronicled on the Swan Tavern bulletin board or pasted on the walls of the taproom. Announcements were put up concerning balls, sporting events, barbecues, lotteries, stage and ferry schedules and rates, and the arrival and departure of ships in the river harbor. Notices were also posted offering rewards for the apprehension of deserting seamen and runaway slaves; traders and slave dealers frequented the tavern exchanging information and gossip relating to recent or proposed slave sales.

The old Courthouse across the street, that for almost one hundred and fifty years had provided such a constant source of patronage for the Swan Tavern, was finally the means of its destruction. During the Civil War the Union forces used the Courthouse for a powder and ammunition magazine; and a letter from Colonel Wister dated December 18, 1863, and contained in the "War of the Rebellion Records," describes the burning of the Swan Tavern when, a day or two before the writing of the letter, the munitions in the Courthouse had blown up. At this time the famous old establishment together with its stable, kitchen, and outbuildings were all completely destroyed.

Ten years after the Civil War, in 1875, the lot was sold to Samuel Brent, who apparently rebuilt some manner of hostelry, for the property became known in court records as the "Brent Hotel lot" until 1905 when it was once more recorded as the "Swan Tavern lot." This later building was also destroyed by fire several years ago, and when the United States purchased the property and the National Park Service took it over there were no buildings standing on the lot.

Exploratory excavations conducted in 1933 by the National Park Service disclosed the ancient brick foundations of the old Swan, its stable, kitchen, and smokehouse. From these physical evidences, Brady Civil War photographs taken before the Courthouse explosion, early insurance records, inventories, etc., all four of the original tavern structures have been reconstructed, the work being completed in 1935.

The Swan Tavern Kitchen has been furnished as a museum display of a typical eighteenth century tavern kitchen and is open for public inspection, as is the reconstructed Swan Tavern Stable which houses an interesting marine museum exhibit of artifacts salvaged from the British ships which were sunk in the York during the Siege of 1781.

At the time of the reconstruction work on the stable in 1935, a new concrete foundation was placed under the old original brick walls to support and preserve them, and during the necessary excavations attending the placing of the concrete, an ancient skeleton was uncovered at one corner of the stable, revealing every evidence by its cramped and doubled position of a hasty burial.

Ye Swan Tavern, 1935
Yorktown, Virginia.

Could it be that long ago the old Swan Tavern yard served as a secret field of honor—that once rapiers crossed at early dawn, resulting in the fate of the unknown who now lies buried at the stable corner? Or was this hurried burial the outcome of skulking figures in the dark of night, a surprise assault, the flash of moonlight on naked steel—and the silence of the grave?

The Nelson House

GENERAL Thomas Nelson, the shining knight of York County, lies as dust in old Grace Episcopal Churchyard, and whether or not his soul is with the saints, his memory will ever remain with those who visit his proud mansion in Yorktown.

Since the Siege of 1781 the Nelson House has been the most pretentious building in town and shall, perhaps, always remain so. One of the best examples of Georgian architecture in all Virginia, the house occupies the southwest corner of Main and Nelson Streets on Lot No. 52, a massive structure of red brick with stone trim, ivy covered walls, and beautifully gardened grounds.

The initial sale of the lot had been made to James Darbisheire by the Town Trustees on July 19, 1699; but he failed to satisfy the covenant to build and forfeited title to the property which then remained with the Trustees until August 2, 1706, when it was conveyed to the first Nelson in Virginia, "Scotch Tom," Yorktown's leading merchant.

The first Thomas Nelson, son of Hugh and Sarah Nelson, left his native town of Penrith in Cumberland County, England, on the

Scottish border and sailed to Virginia, arriving in 1705 to found one of its most illustrious families.

By 1710 he was well established, having acquired several properties in the newly developed Town of York. He married Margaret Read, daughter of John Read, by whom he had two sons, William and Thomas, and a daughter, Mary. He had built his first modest house on Lot 52 and, as business prospered, branched out into other ventures. Besides his warehouse and wharf on the waterfront he, together with Joseph Walker, bought Lot 25 and built the Swan Tavern, which was opened in 1722.

After the death of his wife, Margaret, in 1719, "Scotch Tom" remained a widower until 1723, in which year he took as his second wife the widow Frances Tucker, raising her daughter, Sarah, as one of his own.

Family tradition holds that the pretentious brick mansion, which remains to this day on Lot 52, was begun in 1711. Several travelers described it as early as 1732 in such a manner as would lead us to believe that it was not a new building then. He lived in this structure until his death in 1745. His widow, Frances Tucker Nelson, remained in residence there until her demise in 1766, at which time the house was left to grandson Thomas Jr., William's son. "Scotch Tom's" obituary in the *Virginia Gazette* said of him, "As he lived just, so was he blessed, not only in the Increases of his wealth, but in the comfort of his children, whom he lived to see enjoying the greatest Honours and Preferments. As he lived truly revered and respected, so he died greatly lamented." He lies buried in the Grace Episcopal Churchyard.

"Scotch Tom's" oldest son, William, born in 1711, after being educated in England, returned to spend the rest of his life in Virginia. He married Elizabeth Carter Burwell in February of 1738, the same year in which he was appointed Sheriff of York County. In December of 1738 their son, Thomas, was born, the first of five sons. William Nelson served as Burgess from York County in 1742 and in 1745 was appointed to the Council, later serving as President. He built a large H-shaped brick mansion on Lot 47, which he had inherited from his father, and made it his residence until his death in 1772. The house remained known as "President Nelson's House" until its destruction by the great fire of 1814.

"Scotch Tom's" younger son, Thomas, born in 1716, also served as a member of the House of Burgesses and was appointed Deputy Secretary of the Colony in 1743. Because the Secretary, William Adair, remained in England, Thomas conducted all affairs of the office and was known as "Secretary Nelson." He had inherited from his father several acres of land along the Hampton Road on the eastern boundary of the original Yorktown layout. On this land he built a most imposing house; the Marquis de Chastellus described it as " a very handsome house, from which neither European taste nor luxury was excluded—." The house stood on a prominent site that made it a landmark. During the occupation of Yorktown by the British forces in 1781, Lord Cornwallis made it his headquarters, allowing Secretary Nelson to remain until October 10th when he was given safe conduct to Williamsburg.

President William Nelson fervently shared the political views of his brother, Thomas, and long before the Revolution urged the colonists to cultivate and patronize local industry rather than depend upon the Mother Country for everything. That he practiced his own preachings is revealed in a letter he wrote to a friend in London:

> I now wear a good suit of Cloth of my Son's Wool, manufactured as well as my Shirts in Albemarle, my Shoes, Hose, Buckles, Wigg & Hat etc., of our own Country, and in these we improve every year in Quantity as well as Quality.

As a youth of fourteen William's son, Thomas, was sent to England for schooling, as was the custom among young gentlemen of the time and received his education at Eton and Cambridge. Returning to Virginia in 1761, he married Miss Lucy Grymes of Brandon; and at Nelson House in Yorktown, they entertained all the great dignitaries of the Colony, becoming themselves the social and political leaders of York County. They had eleven children, seven of whom married into the Page family. To distinguish him from his grandfather, "Scotch Tom," and his uncle, Secretary Thomas Nelson, William's son was called "Thomas, Jr."

Through the influence of his family, Thomas, at twenty-one, became a Burgess for York County and was a member of the Continental Congresses of 1775, 1776, and 1777. He represented York County in the Virginia Convention of 1776, offering to that body a resolution that had been written by Edmund Pendleton, calling upon the General Congress at Philadelphia to declare the United Colonies to be free and independent states. The resolution was unanimously passed; and Richard Henry Lee, one of Virginia's delegates, was instructed to present this message before the Congress. The result was the preparation of the Declaration of Independence, of which Thomas Nelson was a signer.

During the Revolution, Thomas was made the third war governor of the new State of Virginia and also served as Commanding General of the Virginia Militia, in which capacity he was with Washington and Lafayette at the Siege of Yorktown.

Lord Cornwallis had at first taken up his headquarters in the house of Thomas' uncle, Secretary Nelson. The exposed location of this house made it a ready target during the Siege bombardment. On the day of surrender, Colonel Tucker wrote in his journal, "The Secretary's house with one of the corners broke off and many large holes thro the roof & walls . . . afforded a striking Instance of the Destruction occasioned by War."

The ruins of the house, still standing a few years after the Siege, were depicted in a water-color sketch by Benjamin Latrobe; and a visitor to Yorktown in 1796 described the house as "in a most shattered condition." The walls were subsequently razed, and in 1927 the site was acquired and marked by a tablet by the Association for the Preservation of Virginia Antiquities.

Several hits were made, and once more the British headquarters were hastily changed, this time to a cave in the river bank. Popular historians, respecting the military prowess of the British Earl, have refused to lend credence to the supposition that he would cower in a cave.

The actual damage done to the Nelson House was repaired long ago but, as mementoes, a couple of cannon balls have been placed in the eastern wall of the building facing Nelson Street.

The Nelsons had been a very wealthy family before the Revolution but gave much of their fortunes as well as their personal services to the cause of the Colonies. General Thomas Nelson went so far as to borrow huge sums personally, over his own signature, to be used in his country's service when he found that many of his lukewarm patriot neighbors were reluctant to lend directly to the newly formed state government. Most governmental debts, they knew, were repaid in Continental script, and while this practice proved the iron lung that saved the Revolution from complete collapse, few colonists would voluntarily exchange sound collateral for this practically worthless paper. The end of the war found Governor Nelson, although still a large landholder, heavily in debt. Indeed, he "gave all for Liberty."

During his triumphal tour of 1824, Lafayette was entertained in the Nelson House by ranking Federal and State officials. The property remained in the Nelson family until 1907 when it was sold to Joseph Bryan of Richmond and was subsequently bought and restored by the late Captain George Preston Blow of LaSalle, Illinois. The Nelson House was acquired by the National Park Service in 1968.

The Edmund Smith House

WHEN the "Towne of Yorke" was established in 1691, the 83 town lots were laid out by the surveyor, Major Lawrence Smith, of Gloucester County. For his services Smith was given Lot 72.

Major Smith had taken part in the Indian wars that followed the 1622 massacre and, as an adherent of Governor Berkeley, led the Gloucester men against Nathaniel Bacon's revolt. As a "Gentleman of Estate and Standing," he had been recommended in 1699 as one suitable for appointment to the Council but was denied enjoying this honor because he died in 1700.

Smith's son, Colonel Lawrence Smith, inherited the Yorktown lot and on February 10, 1706, added to his holdings by buying Lot 53 on the west side of Nelson Street.

Colonel Smith established himself in Yorktown, serving as Sheriff and Burgess from York County. He first married Mildred Chisman, daughter of Captain Thomas Chisman and Elizabeth, daughter of Colonel George Read. Smith and Mildred had three children. When his wife died, Colonel Smith married Mildred Read, daughter of John Read, Colonel George Read's eldest son. By his second wife, Smith had five children.

The original grantee of Lot 53 in 1699 was William Simson who forefeited title by failing to build. Colonel Smith must have erected some sort of building as he retained title until January of 1734 when he conveyed to Edmund Smith, his son and heir, the property described as "joining on one side upon Mr. Thomas Nelson (Lot 52) and on the other side upon Captain John Ballard (Lot 54) and known by the figures 53."

The careers of both Major Lawrence Smith and Colonel Lawrence Smith are treated in more detail in the chapter on the Moore House. The Colonel's son, Edmund Smith, married Agnes, daughter of Richard Sclater of York County and Mary Nutting. They had four children, Mildred, Lawrence, Thomas, and Mary.

Edmund Smith is recorded as having a new house under construction on Lot 53 at the time of his death in 1751. His will, dated the previous 18th of December, gave "unto my Daughter Mildred Smith my Lot of Land in York Town whereon I am now building. It is my will and desire that the House should be finished out of my estate." A later deed "devised Lot 53 to his Daughter Mildred now the wife of David Jameson."

David and his wife, Mildred, leased their new house to James Tarpley, a Williamsburg merchant, on January 17, 1753; but the deal apparently fell through because nine months later the Jamesons were back living in the house.

David Jameson, of Scottish descent, was the son of James Jameson of Essex County in Virginia and was another of Yorktown's successful merchants, as he advertised himself in the *Virginia Gazette* for June, 1751. Besides dealing in the shipment of tobacco and importation of various merchandise, his multiple activities included real estate sales, conducting lotteries, managing a salt works, indenturing servants, buying and selling of slaves, and operating a warehouse on the waterfront. His wife, Mildred, was sister to the Lawrence Smith who apprenticed himself to Jameson "to learn the art of merchantdize and book keeping." The Jamesons lived in the house that Edmund Smith had built on Lot 53 until their deaths; Mildred in 1778 and David, fifteen years later, in 1793.

The Jamesons had other properties in addition to the town house which they had acquired both by inheritance and purchase; one was the old Ludlow Plantation that became Temple Farm and had been bought by Major Lawrence Smith. Mildred was buried in the old Smith family cemetery in the Ludlow Tract on Wormley Creek. At the time of her death, this property had passed to Augustine Moore who had married Mildred's aunt, Lucy Smith. Mildred's tomb may still be seen there, as related in the chapter on the Moore House.

David Jameson distinguished himself, as so many of the successful town merchants did, in a succession of public works, civic offices, and cultural interests. He occupied the office of Treasurer in 1773 and 1774 of the "Society for the Promotion of Useful Knowledge" which he had helped organize at Williamsburg in 1773 together with John Clayton, the botanist, and John Page of Rosewell. One of their experiments concerned the measurement of dew and rainfall with an instrument of their own device said to have been the first of its kind ever used.

During the Revolutionary War, David Jameson served in the Virginia Senate of 1776 and in 1777 was named to Patrick Henry's Privy Council. In 1781 he served as Governor Thomas Nelson's Lieutenant Governor, becoming acting governor briefly during Nelson's illness in August of that year.

As noted in the chapter on the Thomas Pate House, Jameson bought this property on Lot 42 in 1784, after the death of his wife, probably as a rental investment as there is no record of his ever having lived there. He was probably living in Richmond at the time of the 1781 Siege as the Alexander Berthier "billeting" plan of that year would indicate that French troops were quartered in the house on Lot 53 immediately after hostilities.

David Jameson had no children, and upon his death in 1793 his large estate was divided among his three nephews, "John Jameson of Yorktown," "David James of Culpeper" and "David Jameson, Jr. of Caroline." It seems obvious that John Jameson received the house on Lot 53 because an insurance policy of 1796 referred to it as the "home of John Jameson."

John Jameson served with distinction in the Revolutionary War as Captain of the Virginia Dragoons in 1776, Major of the First Continental Dragoons in 1777 and by 1779 as Lieutenant Colonel. Reportedly he was wounded at Valley Forge and participated in the capture of Major John Andre, Benedict Arnold's conspirator, in September of 1780.

In 1815 the house on Lot 53 passed from Colonel John Jameson to Major Thomas Griffin, a participant in the War of 1812 and Congressman from Virginia in 1803-1805. Griffin occupied the house until his death in 1836.

After Griffin's occupancy the house passed through a succession of ownerships until 1915 when George P. Blow of La Salle, Illinois, acquired the property as a part of the "York Hall Estate" which included the Thomas Nelson, Jr. House and the Captain John Ballard House.

The architectural firm of Griffin and Wynkoop was engaged by Mr. Blow to convert the old Edmund Smith House into a guest cottage; changing the original frontage from Nelson Street to the rear garden grounds; adding dormer windows to the rear of the building; and connecting the building to the Nelson mansion by a garden walk.

If it is the old Edmund Smith House, the existing building on Lot 53 is one building in Yorktown for which the exact year of construction is known, based upon Smith's will of December 18, 1750, in which he stated that he was at that time building on his "Lot of Land in York Town."

Architecturally the building is a simple, gabled brick structure of one-and-a-half stories with a full basement half above grade. Exterior chimneys of brick are centered on each gable end. A center doorway on the first floor is flanked by two windows on each side with double-hung sash of eighteen lights. At the second floor, double-hung dormer windows are centered over each opening below. The interior room arrangement has been so altered over the years that the original plan would be difficult to determine.

The Captain John Ballard House

R EFERENCE has been made in the chapter concerning the Dudley
Digges House on Lot 77 that the typical town dwelling house of
eighteenth century Tidewater Virginia was more likely to have been of
frame than of brick construction. Of all the frame houses known to be
in Yorktown during that period only one, other than the Digges House,
remains. It is the old residence of Captain John Ballard on Lot 54,
facing on Nelson Street, which closely resembles the Digges House
and has many a counterpart in Williamsburg.

Thomas Sessions, the carpenter, originally purchased Lot 54 in
1691 but failed to retain title as he failed to erect a structure thereon
within a year of the purchase. The property apparently remained dor-
mant until June 10, 1706, when Edward Fuller, a baker of Hampton
Parish, was granted title to "all that lott or half acre of Land Situate
in York Towne being part of ye Port land there known by ye number
54 as by ye plat on Record doth appeare."

Fuller attempted to convey the lot to Use and Peter Gibson in
exchange for Lot 58, whereon the Gibson brothers had been conducting an ordinary; but this exchange was never carried out because in

1709 Edward Fuller left the lot to his "loving" son Stephen, who in 1720 sold it "with the houses, etc." to John Gibbons. This would indicate that as early as 1720 there was a house on the property.

In 1727 John Gibbons left the property to his daughter, Elizabeth, and her husband, Captain John Ballard, who lived there until 1744.

John Ballard was the son of Lieutenant Colonel Thomas Ballard who had been one of the original Trustees of the Town of York in 1691 and had been given Lot 16 for his services. Lieutenant Colonel Thomas Ballard had served as Sheriff of York County and Justice of the Peace, sitting as Burgess for York County from 1693 to 1711. His father, Colonel Thomas Ballard, had been Clerk of York County in 1652; an Assemblyman for James City in 1666; and a Councilor in 1670, losing his seat because "of his sympathy with and furtherance of the rebellion" of Nathaniel Bacon, Jr.

By 1680 Colonel Ballard had made peace with the Council and was Speaker of the House of Burgesses. In common with "Scotch Tom" Nelson, Richard Ambler, and Philip Lightfoot, Ballard followed the profession of merchant with a warehouse on the waterfront and ownership of several properties in the town including the house on Lot 54. Upon his death in 1745 he provided for his widow, Elizabeth, to remain in the house "during her widowhood for the better enabling her to maintain and bring up their children," sons Thomas, John, Robert, and William and daughters, Catherine and Elizabeth. In the event of the widow's remarriage or death, Thomas was to inherit the house and his father's "gun, pistols, sword and watch."

The widow maintained residence there until her death in 1756, but there is no record of son Thomas ever acquiring title to the house which had become the property of his brother, John, by 1761. In May of that year the brother, Captain John Ballard, who had married Anne Sayer, sold the house to John Thompson, before the Ballards moved to Princess Anne County where the Captain served as Clerk of the Court from 1761 to 1765 and as Burgess in 1766-1768.

John Thompson was also a merchant and one wonders how the little Town of York supported so many men in trade. At any rate, Thompson also prospered so that by 1768, along in years, he was ready to retire and advertised his properties for sale including the house on Lot 54, two lots and houses in Gloucester, a sloop of "about 1800 bushels burthen" and several slaves. He was unable to find a buyer for the Yorktown house, however, until 1773 when it was sold to Thomas Powell, the Yorktown "surgion" and partner of Dr. Corbin Griffin.

Powell had married Colonel Edward Digges' daughter, Elizabeth, in 1772, setting her up in the house on Lot 54 from which he conducted his medical practice for the next three years. With the Virginia Militia occupying the town in 1776 and fear of imminent arrival of British forces, many of the town's inhabitants sought refuge in a safer locale. Powell was one to so desert the town, announcing in the *Virginia Gazette* of May 15, 1776 that: "The present situation of York has occasioned me to remove my family to this Town (Fredericksburg)."

On December 15, 1777, Surgeon Powell sold the house and lot to William Cary, a retail storekeeper, who made it his home until his death in 1805. The house escaped the disastrous fire of 1814, possibly being protected by the Edmund Smith and Thomas Nelson brick houses between it and Main Street.

After Cary's death the house passed through a succession of many ownerships, the Burts, Sheilds, Rubens, Chandlers, and Beers until it was acquired on May 26, 1916, by Captain George Preston Blow of La Salle, Illinois. The house at that time had been owned by Mrs. Lissetta Beer to whom Blow granted life tenureship as a condition of sale. Upon Mrs. Beer's death, Blow converted the house to a caretaker's residence, or sometime guest house, as it was used until sold as a part of the Blow estate to the National Park Service in October of 1968.

The street on which the building faces was originally called Pearl Street and the house, Pearl Hall. In later years the street name was changed to Nelson Street.

The building, sixty feet long by twenty-four feet wide, is a story-and-a-half, weatherboarded, frame construction with a central entrance doorway flanked on either side by two eighteen-light, double-hung window sash; double-hung dormer windows of twelve lights occurring over each of the openings below. The interior plan arrangement has been so altered over the years as to give little indication of the original layout which was probably the typical central hall plan with rooms opening off the hall on either side.

117

The Old Court House, 1818,
Yorktown, Virginia.

The Court House

ACCORDING to the earliest record relating to the holding of court
in York County, the first judicial session was held on July 12,
1633, in the residence of Captain John Utie on his plantation estate
in the Kiskiack country, eight miles above the present site of Yorktown.
In subsequent years courts were convened at the houses of the various
Justices throughout the county. The house of Captain Robert Baldry
at old York was rented for a courthouse in 1658 at an annual rental
of one thousand pounds of tobacco. The rent was later raised to four
thousand pounds which included "entertainment" of the Justices.

Providing entertainment for public officials at the public expense
seems to have been a general practice which, like all good things, was
prone to be taken advantage of. It was one of the sore points that led
in no small measure to the uprising of the last quarter of the seventeenth century under Nathaniel Bacon. After Bacon's Rebellion the
Commission which was sent over by the King to investigate and report
upon the conditions that led to the Revolt, recommended as one relief
to the grievances of the people that the allowances out of the public
monies be discontinued for "liquor drank by any members of committees."

Apparently the worthy Justices were loath to depart from their convivial, convenient, and informal procedures, for it required a special Act of the Virginia Assembly in 1696 to order the holding of court in a regular manner at the "Towne of York." This act was lobbied through the Assembly upon the complaint of diverse inhabitants of York County who bitterly protested that the usual meeting place where court was held was "very inconvenient and remote to a great part of the inhabitants of York County, and may be appointed elsewhere to the greater ease and advantage of the people in general." The Act further provided that "an house suitable and fitt to hold courts in" be erected at the charge of the county within the town limits of York. Five years previously the fifty-acre tract purchased as a town site had been surveyed and plotted off into half-acre lots; and the lot numbered 24, occurring at the northeast corner of the intersection of Main and Ballard Streets, had been reserved for the public use of the county. Upon this site the commissioners elected to build the first courthouse within the town limits; and court has been held ever since in the various structures that have occupied this first selected site. By the next year, 1697, the construction of the house, "suitable and fitt," was well under way. Governor Francis Nicholson hurried the work along with a personal contribution of £5 sterling, and the County Court ordered the Sheriff to remove to Yorktown "ye Standard of this County, ye prisson stocks and pillory" which had been erected two miles down the river at old York in 1661 by Jerrard Hawthorne for eight hundred pounds of tobacco.

Along with the Courthouse a Clerk's Office was built; and with succeeding courthouses, which were built to replace those destroyed by fire or war, new structures for the Clerk of the Court have been constructed. The records of York have been saved and preserved through all the trials and vicissitudes of the county's eventful history. Dating back to 1633 they are, next to those of Accomac County, the oldest records in Virginia. The early records of James City County, wherein is situated Williamsburg, were moved to Richmond during the Civil War for safekeeping. At the evacuation and burning of Richmond the records perished with the flames. The York County records, hidden in an old farm house during the occupation of Yorktown by the Federal troops, were happily saved for the most part, and as Williamsburg was originally part of York County, these old papers and court records have been of priceless value as research material in obtaining necessary data in the restoration of Williamsburg. Among the treasures contained in these early records are papers pertaining to the first Lees to come to Virginia, the last will of Peyton Randolph, and the deed to the site of the first theater in America which was built in Williamsburg.

The establishment of Yorktown as a port for the shipping of tobacco and receiving point for many foreign imports to the Virginia Colony, the influx of a sizable permanent population, and the rapid development of the tobacco culture soon created a demand for more commodious Court quarters. In 1730 several commissioners consisting of Lawrence Smith, who had originally laid out the town, Thomas Nelson, Archibald Blair, William Stark, and Richard Ambler, the Collector of Ports, were appointed to receive proposals for erecting a new courthouse, to be built of brick, twenty-four feet "in the clear," forty-eight feet long, floored with stone from England and to be built at the expense of the county. Thirty-four thousand pounds of tobacco were collected by titheables levied to defray the construction costs.

By the turn of the eighteenth century the Elizabethan and Tudor influences that had marked the early architecture of the colonies had been completely outmoded by the development of the English Renaissance, and the Courthouse of 1730 was perhaps the most imposing building in Yorktown with its "compass head windows," dentil and modillion cornices, and interior panelwork. Early records of repairs made to the various architectural details assure us that nothing was spared to use as many of the classical features finding such favor in England as the purses of the colonists could readily afford.

During the Siege of 1781 the Courthouse was held by the British. Although the structure did not intercept any of the cannon balls of the Allies' bombardment, considerable damage was done to the interior woodwork by the English soldiers. Every window in the building must have been broken either by the British soldiers or the French, who later used the building as a hospital, because upon the termination of hostilities and the subsequent repair of the war's damage to the town's buildings, the county received a bill for "glaising" over two hundred window panes in the Courthouse.

Months after the surrender of Cornwallis, the French soldiers still maintained their hospital quarters in the Courthouse until the town fathers felt their saviour guests had long outlived their welcome.

The newly commissioned Sheriff of the County and the Magistrates decided that the need for a courthouse was great and that they could not "set to do business in any House but the Court House which at present is used by the French as an hospital, the variety of disorders therein, and the disagreeable smell of the house deterring gentlemen from going in."

Perhaps some of the reluctance of the Frenchmen to leave Yorktown may be explained by this excerpt from a letter of one of the town belles, Miss Mildred Smith, to her friend, Miss Betsy Ambler in Richmond:

> The girls here are charming, but there is so much freedom and levity, almost amounting to indiscretion, in their conduct that I often blush for them. . . . Fain would I cast a veil over their frivolities, but since the arrival of the French ships, commanded by the Viscount Rochambeau and Captain M—, their heads seemed turned. . . . There is something so flattering in the attentions of these elegant French officers, and although not one in ten of them can speak a word of English, yet their style of entertaining and their devotion to the ladies of York are so flattering that almost any girl . . . would be enchanted.

Eventually the French departed, and the necessary repairs and reconditioning were effected to restore the building to its original purpose. The structure was used until March 3, 1814, when the most disastrous fire in the history of Yorktown wiped out practically all of the town along the waterfront and destroyed several of the buildings in the town proper, among them the church and the Courthouse, which was almost completely consumed. At the time of the fire British warships were sighted in the Chesapeake, and a legend has persisted that the town suffered bombardment during the War of 1812, but there is no known record that the British ships came up the river and fired on the town. If the possibility of a British bombardment is discounted, the fire was of unknown origin.

A pertinent reference, however, that might indicate the presence of hostile British ships in the vicinity is included in a newspaper account of the great fire that destroyed a large portion of the town on

March 3, 1814. This narration was published in the March 9, 1814, edition of the Richmond *Enquirer*:

> York, March 4.
>
> Yesterday about 3 P.M. Mrs. Gibbons' house in this place took fire, and together with the county Court-house, the Church, the spacious dwelling of the late President Nelson, and the whole of the town below the hill, except Charlton's and Grant's houses, were consumed . . . The lower town was occupied principally by poor people, who are now thrown upon the world without a shelter or a cent to aid them in procuring one. Mr. Nathaniel Taylor and Simon Z. Block are the principal sufferers in amount there — the former finds the result of more than twenty years of honest industry a heap of ruins. The wind was high and the buildings were old — the fire spread, of course, like a train of powder . . . The Dragon 74 (guns) was in sight — a frigate, a brig and a schooner in Mobjack Bay.

These were British ships, and the location places them about twenty miles down the river from Yorktown. The newspaper article concluded with an appeal for funds to relieve the condition of the victims of the Yorktown fire and noted that "A handsome subscription has already been made up—say 4 or 500 dolls."

Arrangements were made in 1816 to rebuild the Courthouse, but it was not until the spring of 1818 that the commission appointed to supervise the rebuilding reported to the Court that it was completed. An insurance record of July 21, 1818, cites the actual value to have been $2,000.00 and the structure to have been a two-story building twenty-eight feet wide and forty-four feet long. It is this structure that is represented in the sketch at the beginning of this chapter.

The building itself was blown to pieces during the Civil War, but the appearance and details of the exterior were fortunately registered before its destruction on the photographic plates of the indefatigable Union photographer, Mathew B. Brady, and have thus been preserved for our study. The sketch was made from one of the Brady photographs showing the front porch piled high with cases of ammunition, bearing out the local legend that the Courthouse had been used by the Union troops as a magazine. The explosion of the stores piled in the Courthouse is mentioned in the War of Rebellion Official Records, and the date is supposed to have been in December of 1863.

While gathering material for his *Pictorial Field Book of the Civil War,* Benjamin J. Lossing visited Yorktown in 1866 and wrote that the Swan Tavern and adjoining buildings (by which he probably meant the Swan Tavern outbuildings, stable, kitchen, etc., and the adjacent Reynolds House on Main Street had been "blown to fragments by an explosion of gunpowder during the war."

The period of Reconstruction was one of little or no development for Yorktown. The shattered community managed without a courthouse until 1875, when a bid to build was accepted, and the building was completed in February, 1876, serving until the erection of the present Courthouse in 1955.

The present Courthouse is so devoid of any historic significance that the portrayal of the 1816 building was considered of more general interest as an illustration to this chapter. The latter edifice, with its simple square pillars and high shaded portico, reflects the strong Greek influence that had supplanted the earlier Georgian-Roman richness of detail. There is something about all of the so-called Federal architecture, tracing from the works of its founder, Thomas Jefferson, that satisfies by its very directness and simplicity of form.

1769
Medical Shop
of Dr. Corbin Griffin,
Yorktown, Virginia

The Medical Shop

JOSEPH G. Baldwin, in 1854, commented upon his countrymen: "One thing I will say for the Virginians—I never knew one of them under any pressure extemporize a profession. The sentiment of reverence for the mysteries of medicine and law was too large for a deliberate quackery."

Yorktown in her finest days had reason to be proud of her eminent sons among the learned professions: her lawyers, engineers, and doctors. But then the true son of Tidewater was inordinately proud of anything and everything pertaining to the section of his nativity. He did not "crow over the poor Carolinian and Tennessean. He does not reproach him with his misfortune of birthplace. No, he thinks the affliction is enough without the triumph. He never throws up to a Yankee the fact of his birthplace. I have known one of my countrymen, on the occasion of a Bostonian owning where he was born, generously protest that he had never heard of it before."

The prestige of Yorktown's doctors was not confined to the town residents. In 1767, the Colonial Governor, who "labored under a very painful and dangerous disorder," sent not for a doctor in Williamsburg, but for Dr. Mathew Pope of Yorktown, under whose ministrations he speedily recovered.

Perhaps the best known practicioner of medicine in Yorktown was Dr. Corbin Griffin, a physician who had studied at the University of Edinburgh in 1765 and was a man of culture and learning, not confining his lore, as was the custom of the day, to "blood-letting, calomel and cathartics."

In 1769 Dr. Griffin owned the Medical Shop that occupied Lot 30 on Main Street, and from his insurance records of that year we learn that it was a very simple, small frame building valued at one hundred dollars. His shop was probably very similar in wares and appointments to other apothecary shops throughout the colonies. Its shelves displayed a wide variety of liniments, purgatives and other remedies with labels that read "Jchlhyocolla," "Rad: Ipeeacuan," "Vin: Rectif: Cong:," "Chaly: of Sulph.," and many more.

Dr. Griffin's library no doubt contained the usual medical books of the day which included Jo. Jonstoni's "Thaumatographia Naturales"; Sharp's "Midwifery"; Shaw's "Physick in two vols."; Burroughs "Physick" and Barbett's "Chirurgery."

After the establishment of Yorktown in 1691, Lot 30 was one of the first pieces of property to be sold. John Rogers was the purchaser on November 24, 1691, and apparently he built on the lot because it remained in his possession until 1706 when he conveyed it to Captain Thomas Mountfort.

When Dr. Corbin Griffin came into possession of the lot there were four structures on it, the shop, a residence, and two small outbuildings. From the residence and shop the good doctor conducted his practice of both medicine and politics. He was an ardent patriot during the Revolution and served as a surgeon in the Virginia line.

The "Boston Tea-party" had been repeated at Yorktown in 1774 when a shipment of tea consigned to the mercantile firm of Prentiss and Co. at Williamsburg arrived in the York. Certain citizens of Yorktown boarded the ship as she lay at anchor and threw the tea into the river. The York County Committee of Safety rebuked Prentiss and Co. as having "incurred the Displeasure of their Country Men." Whether or not Dr. Griffin took part in this adventure we do not know, but it is known that he served on the Committee of Safety for two years.

During the Siege he was taken prisoner by the British, and in a letter dated September 25, 1781, we find his good friend, General Thomas Nelson, angrily demanding of Lord Cornwallis:

"I must request that your Lordship will inform me of the Reason of Dr. Griffin's Confinement on Board of one of your Prison Ships." Whether Griffin had visited the enemy in his professional capacity or had been apprehended in his military capacity is a matter of conjecture. At any rate, with the successful termination of the Siege he was released and lived to serve York County for many years as Justice and also was a Member of the State Senate. He married Mary, the daughter of Colonel Edmund Berkeley, and they had eighteen children, a record even for those days.

Perhaps the good doctor turned to politics after the Siege because of the ruinous condition of the town. The Yorktown shops, stores, and warehouses had been well stocked before Cornwallis came to town, but what the British did not steal was "bought" by the French and American armies after the surrender with practically worthless Continental script. It is very likely that Dr. Griffin found his Medical Shop clean as a bone when the town finally rid itself of the military forces because the army's medical supplies were always low.

Besides listing many eminent practitioners of medicine, the Tidewater claims the first asylum in the world ever devoted exclusively to the care and treatment of the insane, located at Williamsburg. Insanity was a common affliction throughout the Colony, and cases such as the one described in the following newspaper account of 1769, were by no means infrequent:

> Yesterday morning the following melancholy accident happaned near York. One Mr. Thompson having been early out about his plantation affairs, came home when it grew hot, and laid down upon a bed and fell asleep, when his wife (who has long been disordered in her senses and has been several times confined) got an ax with which she struck him on the head and killed him as he lay.

Those intrigued by natural phenonema may make the most of this marvelous occurrence narrated by William Byrd in his accounting of an amazing adventure that proved fatal to a doctor in 1736:

126

A Surgeon of a ship came ashoar at York to visit a patient. When it was almost dark there came a dreadful Flash off Lightening, which Struck the Surgeon dead as he was walking about the Room, but hurt no other Person, tho' several were near him. At the same time it made a large Hole in the Trunk of a Pine Tree, which grew about Ten Feet from the Window. But what was most surprising in this Disaster was, that on the Breast of the unfortunate man that was kill'd was the Figure of a Pine Tree, as exactly delineated as any Limner in the World could draw it, nay, the Resemblance went so far as to represent the color of the Pine, as well as the Figure. The Lightening must have probably passed thro' the Tree first before it struck the Man, and by that means have printed the Icon of it on his breast.

In 1806, the Yorktown Medical Shop was owned by Lawrence Gibbons. He probably took this building over when Dr. Corbin Griffin went into politics. Griffin died in 1813, and a year later the great fire that swept through the town burned the Medical Shop to the ground. The fire, in fact, started in Gibbons' house next to the shop.

The old brick chimney foundations of the shop were located by exploratory excavations in 1935, following the location and dimensions shown on the Griffin insurance records of 1796. Together with these dimensions and the descriptive notes that classified the structure as a building of "wood covered with wood" and also gave the length and breadth of the shop, the location of the door, etc., it was a relatively simple matter to reconstruct the building. This was done by the National Park Service in 1936.

The sketch heading this chapter shows the completed reconstruction of Dr. Corbin Griffin's Medical Shop as it supposedly appeared during the Siege of 1781.

The Old Windmill
Yorktown, Virginia.

Windmill Point

MANY grist mills were established during the Colonial years
along the various creeks and ponds that lie above and below
Yorktown. They were almost universally of the overshot or undershot
paddle wheel type, and there is only one known instance of a windmill
having been built within the county of York in pre-Revolutionary times,
although Sir George Yeardley had introduced windmills into the colony
in 1619 during his administration as Colonial Governor of Virginia,
and at least one windmill was built at Williamsburg.

The most exposed, highest, and logical site for a windmill was on
a pointed bluff just above the town. This site was sold by John Lewis
and his wife in 1711 to William Buckner "for a wind mill" and part
of the sale agreement was the stipulation that the mill should grind
corn. The description of the property in this first record of sale of the
site placed it "at a point near Yorktown . . . just below a small creek,"
tallying nicely with the bluff still known as Windmill Point which lies
at the mouth of, or just below, Yorktown Creek. The windmill is shown
located at this point by the conventional indication of sails and tower
on the Bauman military map prepared at the time of the Siege of 1781.
It is also shown in what apparently is meant to be a view of the same

location in Peale's painting of Washington meeting with the officers of the American and French armies after the surrender of Cornwallis.

An engraving exists showing the mill as it appeared in 1850 in which the structure appears to have been long abandoned. The sails are gone and the building exhibits signs of poor repair.

In preparing the sketch heading this chapter, study was made of existent New England windmills and English mills of the period, especially those of southwestern England from whence emanated so much of the architecture of the colonies. The sails shown are typical of windmills of the early eighteenth century both on this continent and abroad, and the long diagonal boom that revolved the turret with the sails into the wind was usually attached to a dolly or carriage that rolled along the ground yoked to an ox team. The framing was of heavy timbers covered with weatherboarding, and the superstructure was supported by a brick base.

The octagonal mill tower and revolving turret indicated on the engraving of 1850 closely approximate old windmills on Cape Cod, as well as those at Cataumet, Massachusetts and Easthampton, Long Island. It is entirely within the realm of possibility that traveling millwrights, plying their trade up and down the Atlantic seaboard, were responsible for the construction of mills at widely separated points. The greater part of the milling equipment, gears, wheels, etc. of Colonial mills were made of wood, locally, but the main shaft gear and castings were fabricated in England.

A study of about twelve of the still existent grist mills of the Tidewater section of Virginia operated by paddle wheels disclosed that they used the same mechanical principle of gearing the wheels operating the revolving millstones. The construction of the mill houses themselves was almost identical and probably was quite similar to many of the mills throughout the other colonies. Many of the old grist mills are still in operation, although the old wood paddle wheels have been replaced with all metal bucket-type wheels. Water-ground meal from these old mills is a staple commodity in the section.

During the Civil War, Windmill Point was used as an observation station by the Union Army and fortified with trenches and breastworks. If the windmill had not disappeared by that time it was probably destroyed by the soldiers.

A modern residence and the remains of the Civil War fortifications occupy the crest of the point today, and there are no indications left marking the site of the old windmill, although careful excavation would, no doubt, uncover the ancient brick foundations.

The Siege of 1781

IN October of 1781, the Franco-American forces engaged British troops of half their number and, to their immense surprise, defeated them. Neither they nor the world at large have ever gotten over that first surprise. It all happened during the first "War to make the World Safe for Democracy" at the little Virginia hamlet called Yorktown.

The marches and countermarches of Cornwallis and Lafayette and the events that finally induced Cornwallis to dig in at Yorktown (while Washington hurried south, and the Comte de Grasse bent every sail to the north), covered several months; and in fully chronicling the moves of the various pieces in this martial chess game, historians have exhausted reams of paper without giving a very clear picture to the student of what actually happened. What the latter wants to know is why did Cornwallis go to Yorktown in the first place? How was Lafayette able to keep him there until Washington arrived? How was it possible for Washington, from four hundred miles away, without airplanes or motor transportation, to arrive suddenly with practically his entire army; and how did the French fleet, without cablegrams or radio, sail all the way from the West Indies, gaily tack into the Chesapeake, land her troops at the zero hour and have the situation well in hand in the very nick of time? The entire situation had all of the elements of high melodrama, and it is a wonder the Yorktown Campaign has not been made the subject of a dozen movie thrillers.

The American forces in Virginia consisted of two thousand militia and one thousand light infantry under command of the Marquis de Lafayette, who had his hands full combating the British army under Phillips and Arnold without worrying too much about what Cornwallis was doing way down south. His orders had been to defend Virginia and to this object, like the good soldier he was, he directed his entire energy. Learning of the northward approach of Cornwallis, Lafayette made every effort to prevent the British troops already in Virginia from uniting with those of the British Earl coming up through North Carolina; but these efforts were doomed, and the British formed a junction at Petersburg in Virginia. Outnumbered almost two to one, Lafayette wrote from Richmond, "I am not strong enough even to get beaten . . . Were I to fight, I should be cut to pieces . . . Were I to decline fighting, the country would think itself given up. I am therefore determined to skirmish but not to engage too far." This conservative plan he followed to the end and by it saved himself, his army, and the State.

There followed a chase across Virginia with Lafayette keeping just a jump ahead of Cornwallis, who gloated to Clinton in a letter dated May 24th, 1781, "The boy cannot now escape me," referring to the youthful Marquis. But the "boy" did escape him and managed by rapid retreats, marching as often by night as by day, to effect a union with the troops of "Mad" Anthony Wayne who had marched down from Pennsylvania to join him.

To date there had been no real fighting because Lafayette, recognizing his insufficient strength, had kept out of harm's way. Now, however, reinforced by a thousand good soldiers under a gallant general, he turned immediately toward the powerful antagonist from whom he had been in flight, following Cornwallis back to Richmond. From Richmond, Cornwallis planned to continue down the Peninsula to Williamsburg where he intended to spend the summer at that spot, "which is represented as healthy," he wrote to Clinton, "and where some subsistence may by procured." As the enemy moved back Lafayette followed.

132

"Lord Cornwallis is retiring," he reported, "and we are following him." The late pursuer was now the pursued and the Marquis' advance guard generally entered town the day after the enemy had left. Lafayette continued studiously to avoid a general engagement, however, because he felt his troops, mostly militia, were too weak to be a match for the British regulars.

Notwithstanding his superior strength over Lafayette, Cornwallis was convinced that if he was to conquer and hold all of Virginia he must have reinforcements and so advised Clinton that he would wait at Williamsburg until the reinforcements he requested arrived from New York.

Instead of complying with this request, Sir Henry announced that a little campaign of his own against Washington in the North made it necessary for him to request Cornwallis for reinforcements and, Clinton being the superior officer, put his request in the form of an order.

The entire British Army, thereupon, left the summer delights of Williamsburg with a collective sigh and moved on down across the bay to Portsmouth where preparations were made to transport a considerable portion of them to New York. Before they had embarked, Clinton countermanded his orders for reinforcements and instructed Cornwallis to abandon Portsmouth and fortify Old Point Comfort. To understand the reasons that prompted this move we must go back a few months and follow the fortunes of Washington in the north.

No man in the whole of America or in England either, for that matter, would have predicted in the late spring of 1781 that within four short months General Washington in New York and Lord Cornwallis in Carolina would be facing each other at Yorktown in an engagement that was to determine the outcome of the war. Never before during the six long years of this tedious struggle had prospects of victory for the disheartened colonists appeared more dubious. The army had no money, no stores, no munitions, few men. The soldiers, unpaid, starved, ragged, had become mutinous. The following is an extract from Washington's diary, his first entry in May, 1781, five months before Yorktown:

Instead of having magazines filled with provisions, we have a scanty pittance scattered here and there in the different states. Instead of having our arsenals well supplied with military stores, they are poorly provided, and the workmen all leaving them . . . Instead of having a regular system of transporation upon credit, or funds in the quartermaster's hands to defray the contingent expense of it, we have neither the one nor the other; and all that business, or a great part of it, being done by military impress, we are daily and hourly oppressing the people—souring their tempers and alienating their affection. Instead of having the regiments completed to the new establishment, scarce any state in the Union has, at this hour, an eighth part of its quota in the field, and little prospect, that I can see, of ever getting more than half. In a word, instead of having everything in readiness to take the field, we have nothing: and instead of having the prospect of a glorious offensive campaign before us, we have a bewildered and gloomy defensive one, unless we should receive a powerful aid of ships, land troops, and money from our generous allies; and these, at present, are too contingent to build upon.

Opposing Sir Henry Clinton's eleven thousand troops holding New York, General Washington had some four thousand morale-stricken men in the vicinity. Count de Rochambeau had as many more French allies at Newport, Lafayette and Wayne another four thousand in Virginia. These men, plus a few detachments in New Jersey and along the frontier, completed the Franco-American army.

Washington wanted to attack Clinton at New York, but the British strength was beyond the capabilities of Washington and Rochambeau's combined forces, even with naval support. Meanwhile, France had sent a large force under Admiral DeGrasse with orders to stop in the West Indies, then come north to the American coast. When Washington learned that these troops would arrive in the Chesapeake Bay area for a short period in the late summer, he set in motion the plan which would ultimately result in victory at Yorktown.

During this same summer Cornwallis, instructed by Clinton to seize and fortify a port for use by larger British ships during the winter, rejected Old Point Comfort in favor of Yorktown and Gloucester Point. By the twenty-second of August, 1781, his entire army, about seven thousand strong, was concentrated at Yorktown and had begun to fortify their position. Although Lafayette at the time was only a few miles from Yorktown, he did not feel sufficiently strong, without the support of Washington's continentals, to attack the entrenched enemy.

The latter was unwilling to impede the progress of fortifying Yorktown by engaging his troops in other enterprises.

Clinton, busily preparing New York for the supposedly contemplated attack, was distinctly puzzled by the withdrawal of Washington's troops. The moving Continental Army was kept in ignorance of its ultimate destination, and before Clinton had ascertained that they were bound for Virginia, De Grasse had set sail for the Chesapeake with twenty-eight sail of the line, arriving off the Virginia Capes at the close of August. He brought with him 3,300 regular French troops commanded by the Marquis de Saint-Simon and, of almost equal importance, 1,200,000 livres in cash supplied by the Spanish bankers of Havana.

Five days after the fleet of De Grasse had taken position across the mouth of Chesapeake Bay, a British fleet of twenty-two ships under Admiral Graves arrived off the Capes on September 5th. Graves formed a battle line to which the French responded by sailing out into open water and the battle was joined. Maneuvering for position was a slow and unproductive process, and after several hours only half a dozen ships of each fleet had been able to bring their guns to bear. Those ships which were able to engage continued their broadsides for several hours. By nightfall several of the British ships "had suffered so much they were in no condition to renew the action" and the entire fleet withdrew out of range.

The next four days were spent by the two opposing fleets at sea in sight of one another, jockeying for the wind, but with neither admiral pressing an attack. Finally Graves decided that "because of the position of the enemy, the present condition of the British fleet, the season of the year, and the impracticability of giving any effectual succour to General Earl Cornwallis in the Cheaspeake, the British fleet should proceed with all dispatch to New York," which it indeed proceeded to do, leaving Cornwallis to his fate. Paradoxically, this sea battle was decisive because it was indecisive. Washington described the battle in his diary as a "partial engagement with Admiral Graves whom De Grasse has driven back to Sandy Hook."

Washington's troops, after an heroic march from the Hudson to Virginia, joined the French forces at Williamsburg, some fifteen miles from the entrenched British at Yorktown. On the morning of the twenty-eighth of September the combined armies, some twelve thousand strong, marched toward Yorktown. On the night of September 29th, the British left their advanced field works and withdrew to those near the town. The French and American troops were ordered to take possession of these abandoned works. A detachment was sent to the Gloucester shore to prevent escape of the British in that direction.

Red-hot cannon balls from the French batteries destroyed three large transports and two British frigates, the *Guadalope* and the *Charon,* and drove all other British vessels from their posts to the Gloucester side of the river. In the meantime the French fleet had the mouth of the Chesapeake completely blockaded, as shown in the *Carte de la Partie de la Virginie.*

Closer and closer the Allies dug their lines toward the enemy and British redoubts nine and ten were stormed. Cornwallis despaired of holding out much longer. On the night of the sixteenth he made a desperate attempt to escape before surrendering. Under cover of a terrific storm, his troops attempted to cross the river to Gloucester, break through the besiegers there and, by rapid marches, push on to join Clinton at New York. The elements interposed to foil this attempt and prevented half the troops from crossing the river, blowing their boats back to the York shore. At dawn those who had already crossed found their numbers insufficient to win through the besiegers' lines and returned to the opposite shore to resume their old positions in the trenches.

Clinton, meanwhile, sent Cornwallis vague promises of relief and, hoping to divert the Allied armies from the south by menacing the north, employed his time and forces with futile demonstrations at New London and in New Jersey against the four thousand troops that had been left under Major-General William Heath for the purpose of holding Clinton secure during the absence of Washington in Virginia. A definite assurance from Clinton that five thousand troops were leaving New York to relieve the besieged regiments at Yorktown determined Cornwallis to hold on until the promised reinforcements arrived. Day after day passed, and the heavy cannonading of the entrenched French and American armies increased.

We may assume from the following notice posted by James Madison that a nephew of General Washington obtained a very good view of the battle.

I do hereby certify that a Telescope belonging to Dudley Digges, Esqr. which was left in my care was delivered to Major Washington, aid to the Marquis de la Fayette, sometime in June 1781, and that the said Telescope has not since been returned.

Js. MADISON

The fusilier's redoubt, where the famous British Twenty-third Regiment of Foot, known as the Royal Welsh Fusiliers, distinguished themselves, according to Cornwallis, with "uncommon gallantry" was under a constant barrage from the French batteries only a few hundred yards away. Sickness spread throughout the English camp until one-fourth of the men were unable to bear arms, and so many of those "who came three thousand miles to keep the past upon its throne" were giving their lives through sickness "for England, home and duty" that the English general, finally despairing of victory, escape, or deliverance, sent a flag to Washington requesting a suspension of hostilities. "We at that time," wrote Cornwallis, "could not fire a single gun. I therefore proposed to capitulate."

In his letter of October 17th to General Washington the following proposition was presented by Earl Cornwallis:

Sir, I propose a cessation of hostilities for twenty-four hours, and that two officers may be appointed by each side, to meet at Mr. Moore's house, to settle terms for the surrender of the posts of York and Gloucester.

I have the honor to be etc,

CORNWALLIS

In accordance with the English general's request a meeting of commissioners was agreed upon to take place at the Moore House on the right flank of the American lines and just in rear of their first parallel. The British Commissioners appointed were Lieutenant Colonel Thomas Dundas and Major Alexander Ross. They met with the representatives of the French and American forces in the persons of the Viscount de Noailles and Lieutenant Colonel John Laurens early on the morning of October 18th in the front parlor of the Moore House and therein drafted the terms of capitulation which were put into execution the next day when Earl Cornwallis was obliged to surrender to the land and naval forces of America and France.

137

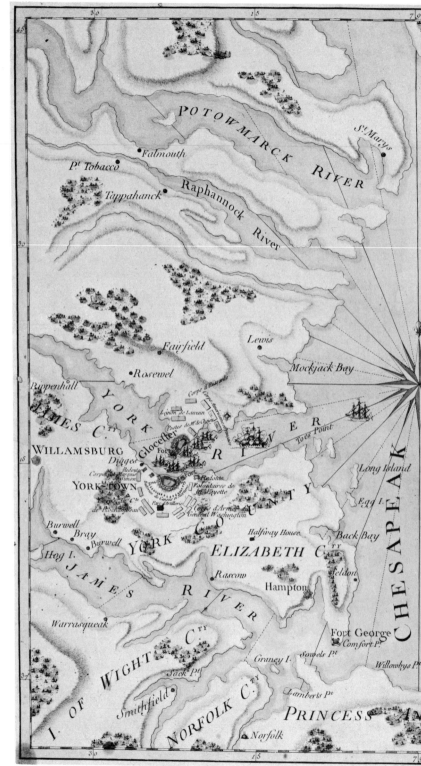

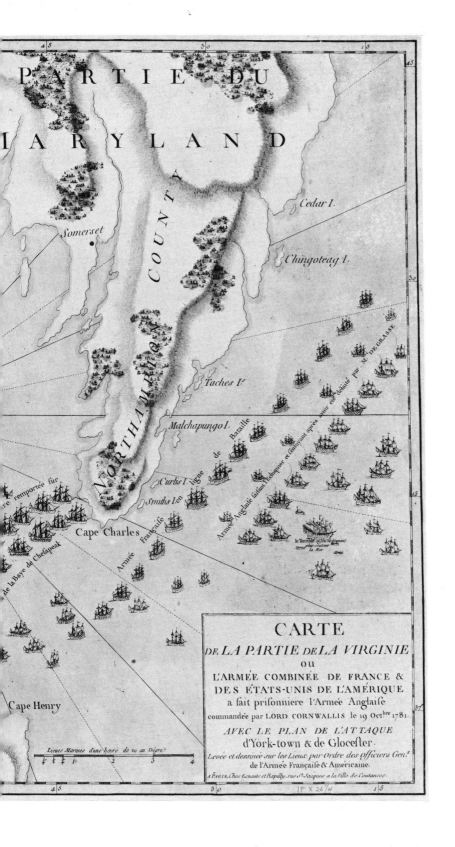

PARTIE DU

MARYLAND

Somerset

NORTHAMPTON COUNTY

Cedar I.

Chingoteag I.

Taches I.

Malchapungo I.

de Bataille

ligne

Curlis I.

Smiths I en

Cape Charles

Armée Françoise

Armée Angloise faisant L'echiquier et s'eloignant apres avoir été déduite par M. DE GRASSE

Armée Angloise

le Terrible entre la gauche plus ouvert de la Mer

re remportée sur

de la Baye de Chesapeak

Cape Henry

CARTE

DE LA PARTIE DE LA VIRGINIE

ou

L'ARMÉE COMBINÉE DE FRANCE &
DES ÉTATS-UNIS DE L'AMÉRIQUE
a fait prisonniere l'Armée Angloise
commandée par LORD CORNWALLIS le 19 Oct.bre 1781.

AVEC LE PLAN DE L'ATTAQUE
d'York-town & de Glocester.

Levée et dessinée sur les Lieux par Ordre des officiers Gen.x
de l'Armée Françoise & Américaine.

A PARIS, Chez Esnauts et Rapilly, rue St. Jacques a la Ville de Coutances.

Lieues Marines d'une heure de 20 au Degré

1   2   3   4

On the very day that the ceremony of the surrender was taking place, the promised relief from General Clinton left Sandy Hook and set sail for the Chesapeake. This armament arrived off the Capes of Virginia five days after the surrender and, receiving news of the capitulation, scuttled back to New York.

The campaign thus developed and successfully terminated was the greatest surprise of the Revolution. After six weary years of indecisive warfare, there was finally created a favorable situation which, supported by the close co-operation of Lafayette's army and the French fleet, offered the long awaited chance for a decisive military success. By suddenly abandoning the proposed attack on Clinton and boldly marching four hundred miles south, General Washington was able to fall upon Cornwallis unexpectedly in a position where succour could not arrive in time to save the British army.

The story of the surrender has been told so often it is common lore to many schoolboys. We are all familiar with the solemn pageant that began three hours after the articles of surrender were signed— how the British army evacuated their works and moved out of their entrenchments as prisoners of war, marched along the Hampton Road where they found the Allied American and French armies drawn up on either side of the way extending for more than a mile toward the field of surrender where each British regiment in turn moved forward and deposited its arms, the final act in this great military drama. Cornwallis sent his second in command, Brigadier Charles O'Hara, to make the formal surrender to General Benjamin Lincoln, appointed by Washington.

Washington's official report reached Congress on the 24th of October, and throughout the land there were celebrations, banquets, and orations. The news of the surrender of Cornwallis was received everywhere with the profoundest joy. Lafayette wrote to the French government in classic drama terms: "The play is over; the fifth act has come to an end." In France, King Louis XVI ordered a "Te Deum" to be sung in the metropolitan church of Paris and requested the citizens to celebrate "with illuminations" the great victory achieved, mainly by French arms, in America.

Even in England the news, while received with resignation, was cause for rejoicing that the long fratricidal conflict was at an end.

Opinion in Parliament rapidly changed after the disaster, and the King was authorized to make peace with America. On November 30, 1782, commissioners from both countries met and signed articles of provisional peace; and on September 3, 1783, the definitive Treaty of Paris was formally ratified.

The long and bitter six-year struggle from Lexington to York-town was finally crowned with success. The Independence of America was achieved, and a new nation was born which was destined to attain a pre-eminent position among the nations of the world.

Glorious Intelligence!

N O R W I C H, OCTOBER 26, 1781.
Friday Evening, Six o'Clock.
By a Gentleman this Moment from New-London we are favoured with the following Hand-Bill.

N E W P O R T, OCTOBER 25.

YESTERDAY afternoon arrived in this harbour, Capt. Lovat', of the schooner Adventure, from York-River in Chesapeake-Bay, (which he left the 20th inst.) and brought us the glorious news of the surrender of Lord Cornwallis and his army prisoners of war to the allied army under the command of our illustrious General, and the French fleet under the command of his Excellency the Count de Grasse.

A cessation of arms took place on Thursday the 18th inst. in consequence of proposals from Lord Cornwallis for a capitulation.----His Lordship proposed a cessation of twenty-four hours, but two only were granted by his Excellency Gen. Washington. The articles were compleated the same day, and the next day the allied army took possession of York-Town.

By this glorious conquest Nine Thousand of the enemy, including seamen, fell into our hands, with an immense quantity of warlik stores, a forty gun ship, a frigate, an armed vessel, and about One Hundred Sail of Transports.

NORWICH:
PRINTED BY JOHN TRUMBULL.

The Moore House,
Yorktown, Virginia.
1769

The Moore House

THE claim to fame of the Moore House relates to an act of peace although its accumulated history was stormy. Within its walls were drawn up the terms of Lord Cornwallis' surrender to General George Washington in October of 1781.

The preceding chapter has endeavored to trace in brief the exciting events of the Yorktown Campaign that led up to the capitulation of the British. Cornwallis, seeking a convenient shelter where his commissioners might meet with the emissaries of Washington and Rochambeau to draw up the articles upon which the surrender was based, found that just to the right of the American lines was a farm house suitable for the purpose. The house was out of the line of fire and had escaped destruction by the bombardment that accompanied the Siege. To it, under proper escorts and flags of truce, repaired the British Commissioners, Lieutenant Colonel Thomas Dundas of the 80th Foot Edinburgh Volunteers and Major Alexander Ross, aide-de-camp and personal friend of Cornwallis, there to be joined by Lieutenant Colonel John Laurens and Second Colonel Viscount de Noailles who represented the American and French forces, respectively.

The four commissioners met early on the morning of the eighteenth of October. Negotiation continued until late in the evening. Sharp argument and heated discussions characterized the meeting. The British Commissioners hesitated about certain terms contained in Article III, which required the British to march out "with shouldered arms, colors cased, and drums beating a British or German march."

Major Ross protested: "This is a harsh article."

"Which article?" said Colonel Laurens.

"The troops shall march out with colors cased and drums beating a British or German march."

"Yes, sir," replied Colonel Laurens, "it is a harsh article."

"Then, Colonel Laurens, if that is your opinion, why is it here?"

"Your question, Major Ross, compels an observation which I would have gladly suppressed. You seem to forget, sir, that I was a capitulant at Charleston, where General Lincoln, after a brave defense of six weeks [in] open trenches by a very inconsiderable garrison against the British army and fleet . . . and when your lines of approach were within pistol shot of our field works, was refused any other terms for his gallant garrison than marching out with colors cased and drums *not* beating a German or a British march."

"But," rejoined Major Ross, "my Lord Cornwallis did not command at Charleston."

"There, sir," said Colonel Laurens, "you extort another declaration. It is not the individual that is here considered. It is the nation. This remains an article, or I cease to be a commissioner."

Before midnight the negotiations ended; the truce was extended until 9 a.m. on the 19th. When he received the commissioners' report, Washington is reported to have made some minor adjustment. The completed articles were dispatched to Yorktown where they were signed by Cornwallis and Captain Thomas Symonds, the senior naval officer. The document was then delivered to the now American-occupied British Redoubt 10, where Washington and his officers waited. There the Commander-in-Chief had another line added: "Done in the trenches before York Town in Virginia October 19, 1781." Then he signed the paper, as did Rochambeau and Barras, the latter for Comte de Grasse of the blockading French navy. At 2 p.m., the defeated British army marched out from Yorktown, their band playing an old British

143

tune, "The World Turned Upside Down." (See appendix for the complete *Articles of Capitulation*).

Many historic sites and structures depend upon legends and folklore unsupported by facts for their continued interest and existence, but the old Moore House at Temple Farm has a wealth of documentary and factual evidence to establish it unequivocally as the dwelling in which the above related meeting of the commissioners took place. Besides being mentioned as the scene of the meeting in every journal of participants of the Siege, it is located and named on the military maps prepared at the time of the Siege by engineers, not only of the American and French Armies, but also by the British.

The Moore House is situated a mile below Yorktown on a section of some of the earliest patented land in all Virginia, lying on the flat of a high plateau that borders the York River from the town to the mouth of Wormley Creek.

The first land along the York was patented by Captain Nicholas Martiau on March 14, 1639 and included the fifty acres that his grandson, Benjamin Read, sold to the county in 1691 to establish the present site of Yorktown. Directly east of the Martiau holdings, George Ludlow obtained patent for 1,452 acres that had originally belonged to the expelled Governor, Sir John Harvey, who had obtained first patent to the land in 1631, "beginning at the mouth of Wormeley's Creek, and from thence running up the River 555 poles unto certain marked trees." It is upon a section of this land that the Moore House now stands.

At the time Martiau patented his land the York was still called the Charles River and the county was called Charles River County. The only settlements along the river were Kiskiack, a few miles above the present site of Yorktown, and old York Plantation, a few miles downstream at the mouth of Wormley Creek. In 1642 the names of both river and county were changed to York and have so remained to the present time.

George Ludlow came out to the wilderness that was Virginia from a prominent family of Wiltshire in England. Except for the tiny settlements of Kiskiack and York he had few neighbors. Just above him was the French military engineer, Martiau, and the hotheaded West brothers had their holdings a few miles beyond that. At Kiskiack was Henry

Lee and immediately above him the adventurous Captain Felgate held forth.

Ludlow soon found his place among his fellows and for many years was a member of the Virginia Council with the rank of Colonel. His sympathies were with the Cavaliers, and in 1649 he entertained the party of political refugees led by Colonel Norwood. When he died his nephew, Lieutenant Colonel Thomas Ludlow became his heir and inherited, besides the land, slaves, and cattle, "113,686 pds. of tobacco, one rapier, one hanger and black belt and one pr. of worn buckskin gloves."

Thomas was soon called to his reward, and with the marriage of his widow to the Reverend Peter Temple, the name of the Ludlow Plantation was changed to Temple Farm, the name it bears to this day, although since Temple's occupancy the estate has changed hands a score of times.

The Temples sold the estate to one "Laurance Smyth." Major Lawrence Smith was a man of great consequence in his day, a mighty Indian fighter, engineer and supporter of the unpopular Royal Governor Berkeley. After leading a "trained band of one hundred and one men out of Gloucester County" in 1675 on an expedition against the Indians near the falls of the Rappahannock, he was selected the next year "as a gentleman that in his time has hued out many a knotty piece of worke, and soe the better knew how to handle such rugged fellows as the Baconians were famed to be." He led his "trained band" out of Gloucester once more against Nathaniel Bacon, the hated enemy of Berkeley, but found his troops more inclined to fight Indians than their fellow colonists. His entire army deserted him in the field and went over to the rebels, preferring to serve Bacon, a man whose usual oath which, according to Berkeley he swore "at least 1,000 times a day, was God damme my blood," a very expressive phrase and somewhat prophetic, too, for also according to Berkeley "God so infested his blood that it bred lice in incredible numbers so that for twenty days he never washed his shirts but burned them."

Ten years later, when the Bacon disturbance was fast becoming a memory, Smith was made Surveyor for the counties of Gloucester and York. In 1691 when Benjamin Read sold the land out of which Yorktown was to be created, it was Major Lawrence Smith who surveyed the tract and plotted it off into the very lots and streets that maintain their original lines and names to this day. The Governor recommended him in 1699 as being among "the gentlemen of estate and standing" suitable for appointment to the King's Council; but he died the next year before he could take office, and the honor deemed worthy of the father was bestowed upon his son, John, who became Councillor and County Lieutenant.

A second son, Lawrence, inherited Temple Farm from his father and also became a prominent person in York County, holding the commission of Colonel and occupying the offices of Justice, Sheriff, Feoffer (Trustee) of Yorktown, and finally became a member of the House of Burgesses at Williamsburg where his obituary appeared in the *Gazette* of that city in 1739 reading, "Tuesday morning last, at his house near Yorktown, died Colonel Lawrence Smith, many years Justice of the Peace and Representative."

The son of Colonel Lawrence Smith, Edward, married Agnes Sclater of York County. Their daughter, Mildred, lies buried at Temple Farm, and her tombstone may still be seen in the family burial plot at one corner of the Moore House gardens. The inscription on the stone reads:

Underneath this marble lies the body of
MILDRED JAMESON,
Wife of David Jameson,
and Daughter of,
Edward and Agnes Smith
Of York County.
She departed this Life
the 10th Day of December, 1778,
in the Forty-sixth Year of her Age.

A second son, Robert, inherited that part of the estate upon which the Moore House is located and sold it to a merchant named Augustine Moore on February 20, 1769. Augustine had married Robert's sister, Lucy, and they were the owners of the Moore House at the time of the Siege of 1781.

Controversy has raged for years over the possible antecedents of Augustine Moore. For many years he was believed to have been the

Moore whom Kate Spotswood, daughter of the Royal Governor, married. Through that possible connection and the finding of broken fragments of a tombstone bearing some of the letters of Spotswood's name at the site of old York near the mouth of Wormley Creek, attempts have been made to link Spotswood with the Moore House. It is now definitely known that Bernard Moore of Chelsea, in King William County, was the spouse of Spotswood's daughter, Anne Katherine. Which still leaves Augustine to be accounted for.

He was probably the grandson of the first Augustine Moore in Virginia, who patented land in 1652, and the son of Captain Augustine Moore who lived in the "old pocoson" precinct in Elizabeth City County, of which he was Justice and High Sheriff in 1697. The Moore families of Elizabeth City, York, and King William Counties, in which the name Augustine appeared to be a family name, were probably all descended from the first Augustine Moore mentioned above. So it is possible that the Augustine Moore of the Moore House on Temple Farm was distantly related to Governor Spotswood through the King Willam branch of the family. However, as Spotswood died twenty-nine years before Augustine bought Temple Farm and built the Moore House, there is no basis for associating the Governor's name with the house. Alexander Spotswood was overtaken by his fatal illness in Annapolis, Maryland in 1740, and it is hardly likely that his body would have been brought all the way back to old York for burial.

The legend connecting the name of Spotswood with Temple Farm started with a letter written in 1845 by the Reverend William Sheild to Bishop Meade and is here reproduced from its printing in Meade's "Old Churches and Families of Virginia":

> I purchased the farm in 1834, at which time the walls of the Temple, from which the place takes its name, were several feet high; within them (after removing the ruins) I found heaps of broken tombstones and on putting the fragments together, to ascertain, if possible, the names of some of the persons who had been buried there, I succeeded in finding the name of Governor Spottswood, showing that he was buried at Temple Farm, a fact, perhaps not generally known.

The fragments of tombstone mentioned by Mr. Sheild in his letter to Bishop Meade have long since disappeared and the legend of Spotswood and the Moore House, thus scrutinized, becomes little more than a pleasant myth.

Another legend that has persisted for many years in modern times is that the old Ludlow Plantation received the name Temple Farm from the ruins of the old church built at York in 1642 before the creation of Yorktown. The early colonists brought the Church of England to Virginia and did not usually call their houses of worship "temples," but churches. Even though some of the Revolutionary War maps do show a tower-like indication at old York labeled "Temple," it is much more likely that the name derives from the early owner, Peter Temple.

Many early accounts of the Siege refer to the house at the time of the surrender as the "widow" Moore's house, but Augustine did not die until 1788, seven years after the Siege. He died without issue and left the estate to his "ever worthy friend, General Thomas Nelson" subject to the life tenureship of Lucy Moore, his wife.

With the death of Augustine's widow the house passed through a succession of ownerships and was occupied as a dwelling until the Civil War, when it was badly damaged.

When the Confederates evacuated Yorktown on May 4, 1862, retreating to their secondary defenses at Williamsburg, the old Moore House was left to the devices of the victorious foe and remained in the hands of the North until the end of the war. In the severity of the winters during the Northern occupation, much of the original structure fed the soldiers' bivouac fires. The doors, window sash, shutters, fences, and as many of the weatherboards as were within easy reach were destroyed in this manner. A photograph taken by the Union Army photographer, Mathew Brady, in the summer of 1862 shows a great deal more left of the house than a photograph taken from the same location by Gardner the following spring of 1863, testifying to the above statements. The solid old timber framing, tenoned and pinned, resisted such efforts and remains sound and in place to this day.

With the close of the Civil War, the Moore House fell into that melancholy state of desolate emptiness so typical of many fine examples of Colonial architecture in Virginia ravaged by the war. It served for a time as a cow barn and was occasionally occupied by transient Negro farmers.

The South, badly crushed by the Reconstruction period that fol-

148

lowed the war, busied itself with the sheer necessity of making a living; and the Moore House with its generous contributions to the pages of American history was well nigh forgotten.

In 1881 came an awakening when Congress gave the War Department an appropriation to prepare the Moore House and its grounds for the Centennial Celebration of the Surrender of Cornwallis.

The repairs made to the building at that time were not considered in the light of a restoration. All vestige was gone of the six outbuildings shown on a map prepared for Rochambeau in 1871. However, we can imagine them to have been the typical smokehouse, dairy, corncrib, well, barns, and stables of the period and locale. To accommodate the functionaries of the 1881 Celebration, a dining-room was added to the building and the alteration necessary to prepare the building for public inspection was embellished with trim and detail of the Victorian era.

After the Centennial the house was again tenanted, and its occupant added another wing of two stories. The house was in this condition when Congress passed the Cramton Bill in 1930 establishing Yorktown and its environs as part of Colonial National Monument. The Moore House, included in this project, was purchased by John D. Rockefeller, Jr. and presented to the United States Government to be taken over by the National Park Service, Department of the Interior.

When the Sesquicentennial of the Surrender of Cornwallis was celebrated in October, 1931, visitors witnessed a three-day spectacle. A large portion of those thousands made the pilgrimage to the Moore House over the road that winds through the still existent British, French, and American earthworks (then serving as bunkers for a golf course). There they listened in awed respect as historians related to them the glorious part the old building had played in our country's early history.

When the captains and the kings had departed, and all expenses had been paid, the Sesquicentennial Committee found that their treasury registered a neat surplus. They unanimously decided to devote these monies to a careful and authentic restoration of the Moore House. The services of the architectural firm commissioned by John D. Rockefeller, Jr. to have charge of the restoration of the buildings in Williamsburg were offered *gratis* to prepare the necessary drawings and details.

After many months of research and study by the historians of

149

the National Park Service, the accumulated research material was turned over to the architects; and based upon this information, photographs, and early engravings of the buildings and the actual physical evidence of the remaining structure, plans and detailed drawings for the restoration work were completed. A construction crew was engaged and began work to bring back the appearance of the Moore House as it was during the stormy autumn of 1781.

With the demolition of the modern wings, the original plan was re-established with its central stair hall from which all of the first floor rooms are centered. According to legend the Articles of Surrender were drawn up in the northwest room of the first floor.

The structure is of wood frame construction with handsome brick chimneys at either end. The roof is framed gambrel style, and the original framing of pine and poplar was found in good condition except for a bit of patching where cannon balls had made passage during the Siege of 1862.

While gambrel roofs were common in Virginia during the eighteenth century, the Moore House roof has an unusual treatment in the snubbing or hipping of the gable ends of the gambrel that is not usually found in that section, although many of the straight gable roofs were so framed throughout the Tidewater country.

Several earlier structures preceded the erection of the Moore House, as excavations conducted at the time of the restoration work of 1933-34 have disclosed foundations for at least three supposedly seventeenth century buildings. Beyond the size and proportions indicated by these exposed crumbling brick and marl foundation walls, no known record exists as to their original appearance. Upon the site of marl foundations for what was probably an early kitchen building, a small building has been reconstructed of marl to house the heating plant for the Moore House. This work was probably the first use of marl for building purposes since those long-gone Colonial days.

It is most fitting and proper that, because of its great pertinent historic interest, the Moore House will be preserved for posterity. The building is now one of the museums of Colonial National Historical Park and is administered by the National Park Service. Uniformed guides are in attendance and the building is open to visitors.

The Victory Monument

THE present Victory Monument is the third and largest memorial to be erected commemorating the successful termination of the Siege of 1781.

The first commemorative shaft was raised at the actual site of the surrender which had been marked with a stone cairn and four poplar trees by William Nelson, son of the Revolutionary governor. According to the records, it was composed of a white marble shaft superimposed to a height of thirteen feet upon a double base of native granite quarried along the upper James River and was erected in 1860 by the 21st Regiment of Virginia Militia "to mark the spot of the surrender of Cornwallis' sword." During the Civil War the monument disappeared piecemeal into the souvenir haversacks of the soldiers of both armies.

The second monument, almost forgotten although still standing, also purposes to mark the spot of the surrender. It is fashioned in the conventional, pointed-shaft style of the 1890's when it was erected, and rises above a stepped base to a height of about ten feet. A certain

151

Mr. Shaw, one time custodian of the National Cemetery at Yorktown, had this second tribute erected at his own expense on a site supposedly marked at the time by the stumps of the four poplar trees planted by William Nelson.

There can be little doubt about the actual locale of the surrender because the field in which the British laid down their arms is plainly marked on several of the military maps prepared at the time of the Siege, and the actual surrender scene has been recorded by eye witnesses.

According to one description of "the most glorious day" as penned in his diary by Dr. Thatcher, a surgeon of the Continental Army, the combined Allied armies lined either side of the Hampton Road for more than a mile with General Washington at the head of the American forces on the right side of the road and Count Rochambeau at the head of the French troops occupying the left. With both lines facing the road the center would have been the "head" and consequently Washington, represented by General Lincoln, accepted the surrender of Cornwallis in the person of General O'Hara at a point something more than half a mile from town or approximately at the site of the aforementioned second memorial shaft of Mr. Shaw. From this site the British Army was conducted into a spacious field where it was intended they should ground their arms. This field, indicated on the Siege maps, is now known and marked as Surrender Field.

According to the eminent historian, B. J. Lossing (who, when gathering material for his *Pictorial Field-book of the Revolution* in 1848, visited William Nelson, grandson of Governor Nelson), "It is the opinion of Mr. Nelson and other intelligent gentlemen at Yorktown that the large field is the locality where the captive soldiers laid down their arms, and where the marble column ordered by Congress, should be erected."

The order of Congress referred to by Mr. Lossing was in the form of a resolution passed on October 29, 1781, by the first Congress to meet after the surrender, providing for the erection of a monument at Yorktown to commemorate the victory. After taking exactly one hundred years to brood over the matter, Congress failed to share the opinion of the earlier Yorktown intelligentsia. When the former august body, after its century of mulling, finally stirred into its customary ponderous motion, the result was an appropriation of $100,000 and a monument erected high on a bluff overlooking the York River just one mile from the scene of the surrender.

In 1880 a joint committee of the two Houses, consisting of one member of each House from each of the original thirteen States, was appointed to provide for the proper celebration of the Centennial Anniversary and to select a site for a monument in commemoration of that event.

The first site selected was on Temple Farm, fifteen acres of which were proposed to be donated to the United States for the purpose. A survey was ordered made of this location in June of 1881 and was subsequently made. On July 7 of the same year, however, plans were changed and the site now occupied by the monument was decided upon and purchased. The ground was covered with Confederate trenches and fieldworks built by General Magruder, and it was necessary for the government to level them off in preparing for the foundation. The site was selected because of its scenic location, commanding as it does a magnificent view up and down the York River. It is of ironic interest to learn that the site thus selected once belonged to the family of Nathaniel Bacon, the seventeenth century leader of organized rebellion against the British Crown.

Three artists were appointed to execute the memorial, R. M. Hunt, J. A. Ward, and Henry Van Brunt; and their design and model were accepted by the Secretary of War in 1880. In the presence of President Arthur the cornerstone of the monument was laid on October 18, 1881, the first day of the four-day Centennial celebration which was attended by thousands, including many invited foreign dignitaries.

The ceremony attending the laying of the cornerstone was conducted by the Masonic Grand Master of Virginia assisted by the Grand Masters of the thirteen original States. Amid much pomp and circumstance, the chanting of hymns and singing of patriotic songs, martial music by the United States Marine Band conducted by John Philip Sousa, many orations and the recitation of considerable poetry, the cornerstone was duly and officially laid.

Flanking the path leading to the monument, two bronze tablets recording the names of the French and American soldiers "who made the supreme sacrifice in the Yorktown Campaign, 1781" were erected by the National Society of the Daughters of the American Revolution on October 19, 1931, the sesquicentennial anniversary of the surrender.

Excavations conducted by the National Park Service in their field studies preparatory to restoring many of the revolutionary earthworks have uncovered several skeletons within the British lines indicating that many of the besieged were buried where they fell. None of these graves were marked, and it is thus very difficult to identify them although their regiments may be fairly accurately determined. Many of the French dead are buried at a site still called the French Cemetery to the west of Surrender Field, and more than 150 soldiers who died during the campaign lie buried in the garden of the Governor's Palace in Williamsburg.

A tombstone found in the basement of the Moore House obviously related to another victim of the Siege, John Turner, a Yorktown merchant who wandered out to view the bombardment and met the usual fate of the innocent bystander. His wife tells the tale in the epitaph on his tombstone:

In Memory of
JOHN TURNER
who departed this Life
October the 13th
in the Year of our Lord
1781
Aged 30 Years

Ah cruel ball so sudden to disarm
And tare my tender husband from my Arms
How can I grieve too much what time shall end
By Mourning for so good so kind a friend.

John Turner may have been a member of the Virginia Militia, but his name is not among those listed on the D. A. R. memorial tablets, the only Turner so listed being Mattocks Turner of Delaware.

The Victory Monument itself is a grotesque design in white marble containing a surprising number of unrelated forms circling, truncating, and surmounting a ninety-five foot star-studded shaft (supported by thirteen female figures representing the original States) above whose composite capital the Goddess of Liberty balanced uneasily with outstretched arms. The work cost the Federal Government $100,000, a considerable portion of which no doubt was expended upon the chiseling of the inscriptions of more than two hundred and seventy words which cover the four sides of the pedestal base, the gist of which may be briefly summed up in these certain few words of the rambling text: "Erected . . . to commemorate the victory by which the independence of the United States of America was achieved."

In 1942 the Liberty Goddess was decapitated by lightning. Rather than repair and restore the original statue, the sculptor, Oakar J. W. Hansen of Charlottesville, Virginia, was commissioned to create a new figure. The new work was mounted on the column on September 10, 1956, and a lightning rod was installed down the core of the shaft. As a part of the Yorktown Day program of the 350th Anniversary of Jamestown, the monument was rededicated on October 19, 1957.

In Memory of
JOHN TURNER
who departed this Life
October the 13th
in the Year of our LORD
1781.
Aged 30 Years

Ah cruel ball fo fudden to difarm
And tare my tender hufband
from my Arms
How can I grieve too much
what time fhall end
By Mourning for fo good
fo kind a friend.

155

Gen. John B. Magruder
"Prince John"

Gen. George B. McCellan
"Little Mac"

The Peninsular Campaign of 1862

FORT Sumter fell on April 13, 1861, and upon the news reaching Washington, President Abraham Lincoln convened Congress and issued a proclamation calling forth 75,000 three-months militia from the northern states to suppress any further military operations against the government. Virginia seceded on April 17th, seized Harper's Ferry Arsenal on the 18th, and the United States Navy Yard at Norfolk on the 20th. On the 19th of April a mob in Baltimore assaulted volunteers as they passed through Washington, burned bridges and cut off railway communication between Washington and the North.

On the night of May 23rd, Confederate pickets were within sight of the Capitol, and the Federal situation was one of alarm. Volunteers who had hastened to Washington upon call of the President were encamped north of the Potomac but had not been formed into regiments and brigades or outfitted for the field. What regular troops were available were dispatched across the river forming a line from Alexandria to the chain-bridge above Washington, under command of Brigadier General Irwin McDowell, a protege of General Winfield Scott, General-in-Chief of the Union forces. By the first of June, the Confederate capital was relocated in Richmond, and the capitals stood defiantly confronting each other with McDowell opposed by an army under command of his old classmate, General Pierre G. T. Beauregard.

President Lincoln, who had had only brief experience in military service, was without knowledge of military affairs or personal acquaintance with military men. His primary concern was the defense of Washington, and he was dependent on the advice of the aging General Scott, in his 75th year at the outbreak of the War. As Secretary of War, Edwin M. Stanton meddled continuously in the planning strategy and issued orders which relieved and replaced commanders in the field most capriciously.

Jefferson Davis, at the head of the Confederacy was, on the other hand, an experienced leader; a graduate of West Point, he commanded a regiment in the Mexican War; was Secretary of War under President Pierce and Chairman of the U.S. Senate Military Committee at the time he left Congress to cast his lot with the South. Davis was not only thoroughly versed in everything relating to War but was well informed concerning the character and ability of all the senior officers on both sides of the struggle. There was nothing haphazard or probational in his selection of commanding officers, and almost without exception, those appointed at the beginning of the War retained their commands until they were killed in battle or the War ended. In addition, Davis had as his military advisor and Commander-in-Chief, General Robert E. Lee. Lee was a native Virginian in the prime of life at age 55, with thirty-five years of continuous service in the regular army of the United States, which gave him the advantage of long acquaintance with his subordinate officers. Appointed Commander of the Army of Northern Virginia on June 1, 1862, to relieve General Joseph E. Johnston who had been wounded at the two-day Battle of Fair Oaks (or Seven Pines), Lee continued as its commander throughout almost the entire War. Contrast this arrangement with the constant replacement of the Union commanders: General Scott by McDowell; McDowell by McClellan; McClellan by Pope and Burnside; Burnside by Hooker; Hooker by Meade; Meade by Halleck; and, finally Halleck by U. S. Grant.

In July of 1861, Lincoln charged Major General George B. McClellan with the responsibility for organizing a large force to defend Washington and march upon Richmond. All through the fall and winter of 1861 McClellan, the young 34 year old general, fortified the approaches to Washington, drilled, reviewed, and inspected his growing army. But he did not move south of the Potomac. When General Winfield Scott retired on November 1, 1861, McClellan succeeded him as Commander of all the Union armies, except the Department of Virginia.

Finally Lincoln, losing patience late in January of 1862, issued General War Order Number I, directing that on February 22nd there should be a general movement by both Army and Navy against the enemy, expecting that his General-in-Chief would move into northern Virginia. Instead, McClellan proposed to approach Richmond by way of Chesapeake Bay and either the York or the James River, a plan Lincoln reluctantly accepted. McClellan assigned sufficient troops for the immediate defense of Washington and the Shenandoah Valley, planning to transport his remaining forces, which numbered 110,000 men, by water rather than overland to Fort Monroe on the peninsula between the James and York rivers.

Union naval forces assigned to support McClellan's operation, reduce the batteries at York and Gloucester, and open up both the York and James rivers consisted of the frigates *Congress, Minnesota, Roanoke,* and *St. Lawrence* and the sloop *Cumberland.* They were to rendezvous in Hampton Roads and await the arrival of the experimental iron-clad *Monitor*, steaming down from New York, before closing with the Confederate iron-clad, *Virginia,* that controlled entrance to the James River.

The Confederate leaders, anticipating the selection of the peninsula and the James River as an invasion route to Richmond, erected strong earthworks at Yorktown protected by seventy guns taken from the Norfolk arsenal. There were additional entrenched positions at Young's Mills on the Newport News Road, at Big Bethel, Howard's Bridge, Ship's Point, and at Williamsburg. The officer entrusted with the responsibility for defending the peninsula, or at least slowing the advance of the Union troops, was Major General John Bankhead Magruder.

On March 9, 1862, the overture to the Peninsular Campaign was sounded by the guns of a naval battle in Hampton Roads where the York River empties into Chesapeake Bay; a battle that was to electrify the world and change all of the rules of naval warfare. On this date for the first time iron-clad vessels met in combat.

In the spring of 1861, Norfolk and its large naval establishment had been abandoned by the Federals, after it was partly destroyed and a large number of ships had been burned and sunk. One of the sunken ships was the wooden frigate *Merrimac* which was raised, converted to an iron-clad, and renamed the *Virginia*.

In January of 1862, Colonel John Taylor Wood was ordered to raise a crew to man the *Virginia*. In the old United States Navy the majority of the officers were from the South, and almost all of the seamen were Yankees from the New England ports. Southern men had flocked to the army, and in hopes of securing some men who had experience as seamen or gunners from the two New Orleans battalions under General Magruder's command at Yorktown, Wood prevailed upon the General, short-handed as he was, to parade his troops in each camp and ask for qualified volunteers. In this manner, Wood obtained some 200 volunteers from whom he selected 80 to serve his purpose, manning the *Virginia's* ten guns and sailing the ship.

The *Virginia* was completely rebuilt from the old berth deck upward with a new mid-section built with sloping bulkheads of pine and oak 24 inches thick covered with overlapping iron plates two inches thick and eight inches wide. On March 8th, the *Virginia* steamed down the Elizabeth River and headed for the Yankee fleet anchored off Fort Monroe. By the day's end she had sunk the sloop *Cumberland* which had thirty guns, forced the surrender of the frigate *Congress* which had fifty guns, and run aground the frigates *Minnesota, Roanoke,* and *St. Lawrence.*

At nightfall the *Virginia* lay off Sewell's Point under the protection of the Confederate batteries, intending to finish off the stranded Federal vessels the next day. The burning *Congress* blew up during the night.

At daybreak of May 9th, a strange looking craft was discovered between the crippled *Minnesota* and the *Virginia*. It was John Ericsson's *Monitor*, the peculiar single turreted, iron-clad craft that had been expected at Hampton Roads ever since its launching on January 30, 1862, at the Thomas F. Rowland Shipyard, Greenpoint, Brooklyn. The *Monitor*, described by some as a "cheese box on a raft," left New

York on May 6th, arriving at Hampton Roads at the most auspicious moment on the morning of the 9th just in time to prevent the *Virginia's* resumption of attack on the grounded Federal ships.

The engagement which then took place between the *Monitor* and *Virginia* (or the *Merrimac*, as the North insisted on calling her) lasted for eight hours at close quarters, each ship maneuvering for position; the *Virginia* attempting to bring her ten guns to bear while the *Monitor* did likewise with her armament of only two. The physical condition of the officers and men of the two ships was in striking contrast. The crew of the *Virginia* had passed the night quietly enjoying rest and sleep while tied up off Sewell's Point; whereas, the *Monitor's* crew had hardly closed their eyes in sleep during the previous forty-eight hours. The *Virginia's* phenomenal success of the previous day had her crew keyed to a high state of morale; whereas the *Monitor's* efficiency in action was yet to be proved. After continuous action of eight hours, the exhausted crew of the *Monitor* withdrew their ship to the shallows of Middle Ground where, because of her deeper draft, the *Virginia* was unable to follow. The action historically is considered a drawn battle. The *Virginia*, although much more seriously damaged than the *Monitor*, still claimed victory because of her exploits the previous day and because the *Monitor* had been the first to withdraw from the contest. The crew of the *Monitor* likewise claimed the victory as they had foiled the attempt of the *Virginia* to complete the destruction of the Union fleet in Hampton Roads; they had remained on station at Middle Ground while the *Virginia* had "retreated" back to Norfolk to assess and repair her damage, leaving the *Monitor* in possession of the field.

For the next two months the situation remained static; the repaired *Virginia* protecting the James River, the *Monitor* guarding the Chesapeake and York River. Neither side had an iron-clad in reserve, and neither wished to bring on an engagement which might disable its only armored vessel in those waters.

On April 2, 1862, General McClellan arrived at Fort Monroe on the tip of Virginia's Tidewater Peninsula. His dilatory tactics and overestimation of the opposing forces have been blamed for the subsequent failure of the campaign, but a good share of his lack of success was due to Stanton. Enroute to Fort Monroe, McClellan had been relieved of general command of the Union armies, his forces being confined exclusively to the Department of the Potomac. On April 4th the First Corps was also withdrawn from his command. Instead of the much larger force upon which his plans had been based, McClellan found his total complement did not exceed 92,000 of whom some 7,000 were unfit for duty due to sickness; an additional 17,000 made up the non-combatants assigned to camp, depot, and train guards, escorts, cooks, servants, and orderlies reducing his effective fighting force to 68,000.

Supplies and wagons to transport them were slow in arriving. Lack of transportation and the condition of the roads held his forces at Newport News for the better part of April.

Included in McClellan's plan for the "general movement by both Army and Navy," as directed in Lincoln's General War Order Number I, had been the reduction of the Confederate batteries on the James, and at York and Gloucester, by Union gunboats. The major part of the Federal fleet in Hampton Roads had been destroyed or run aground by the iron-clad *Virginia* that still controlled entrance to the lower Chesapeake and James River. McClellan was advised by Commodore Louis M. Goldsborough, USN, that the Union Navy could consequently supply no water support, and the slow movement up the peninsula was begun overland.

The strategy of the opposing forces can best be understood knowing the character of the opposing generals: McClellan, the politically ambitious, but cautious engineer; Magruder, the professional militant with years of commanding troops in the field.

The Philadelphian, George Brinton McClellan, entered West Point as a child prodigy at the age of fifteen, the youngest cadet ever to enter the Academy, an exception having been made in his case as he had already completed two years at the University of Pennsylvania. Nicknamed "Little Mac" at the Point, he graduated in the upper ten per cent of the class of 1846 and served with distinction in the Mexican War.

McClellan was known throughout the service for the painstaking, meticulous care with which he organized the various expeditions and explorations for which he was responsible. He would never move until the last item of equipment had been received and the most insignificant detail arranged to his complete satisfaction.

161

John Bankhead Magruder, the dashing, wealthy, social lion from Virginia, had earned the soubriquet "Prince John" during the Mexican War where he had also served with distinction. His gaudy uniforms and the splendor of his regimental mess became legendary as were his courage and daring.

A spit-and-polish officer and rigid disciplinarian, while serving as commanding officer of the San Diego garrison in 1853, he had earned a dubious reputation by ordering the hanging of three of his soldiers, the first such execution to take place during peace time in the history of the U.S. Army.

Thus it was that the opposing forces of these two West Point classmates and brothers-in-arms during the Mexican War faced each other from opposite sides of the Yorktown defenses.

Adding to McClellan's problems were his unfamiliarity with the country, the faulty maps and intelligence provided by Pinkerton's secret operatives, and the unseasonable rains that turned the clay roads into quagmires requiring endless delays in corduroying the roads with logs. The many swamps and unbridged and unfordable streams, that were not indicated on any maps, made the eventual retreat of Magruder's forces almost as difficult as McClellan's advance.

Despite these multiple disappointments and frustrations, it must still be admitted that McClellan's available troops far exceeded in numbers the opposing Confederates who mustered some 15,000 under Magruder at Yorktown and about an equal force at Norfolk under Major General Benjamin Huger. McClellan's delay in moving on up the peninsula allowed General Lee to send down reinforcements from Richmond so that by May 1st the Confederate strength manning the Yorktown fortifications was some 36,000 men.

Throughout military history, victory has not invariably fallen to the side favored with the most men. According to what Cyrus says, in *Xenophon*, "It is not the number of men but the number of *brave* men that gives the advantage, the remainder serving rather as a hindrance than a help." Experience in battle makes for brave troops. The majority of McClellan's troops were raw recruits with only a few months in the training camps and untested in battle.

On April 12th, 1862, Magruder was replaced by General Joseph E. Johnston, Magruder retaining command of the right sector of the

Yorktown line. Keeping McClellan's preparations for the siege under constant surveillance, Johnston became convinced that once the Yankee siege guns were in place his own position would be rendered untenable, and proposed in a dispatch to President Davis the evacuation of both Yorktown and Norfolk. He received the following reply:

Richmond, Va., May 1, 1862

General J. E. Johnston,

Yorktown, Va.

Accepting your conclusion that you must soon retire, arrangements are commenced for the abandonment of the Navy Yard and the removal of public property both from Norfolk and this Peninsula.

Your announcement to-day that you would withdraw tomorrow night takes us by surprise, and must involve enormous losses, including unfinished gunboats. Will the safety of your army allow more time?

Jefferson Davis

Johnston ordered the evacuation of the Yorktown defenses for May 3rd, but heavy rains and conditions of the roads delayed this action until May 4th when the Confederate forces, under cover of a heavy storm, fell back to their secondary defense line at Fort Magruder on the outskirts of Williamsburg, abandoning at Yorktown seventy pieces of heavy ordance as the price of their retreat, and yielding the entire Yorktown line to the Federals without further resistance.

Deciding against immediate frontal attack, McClellan had elected to employ siege tactics, digging in until his heavy artillery could be brought forward. This procedure was in strict accordance with accepted military doctrine that dictated the use of superior forces in attacking a well fortified position, the attack to be preceded by a heavy concentration of artillery fire. That this tactic proved successful was borne out by subsequent events. His batteries were in position by May 5th at which time, according to his own account, he had some 42,000 men in position for the assault after the opening bombardment.

The Northern invaders had been at bay below Yorktown for nearly a month while the small rebel force, under Magruder, by skillful tricks and maneuvers, so deceived McClellan as to the number of the enemy opposing him that Yorktown was regularly besieged, much to Magruder's amusement. The latter, describing his strategy, wrote in a letter dated May 3, 1862, "Thus . . . we stopped and held in check over one hundred thousand of the enemy. I was much amused when I saw McClellan, with his magnificent army, begin to break ground before miserable earthworks (at Yorktown) defended by only eight thousand men". There were actually 36,000 in the Confederate lines.

While McClellan and Magruder carried out classic maneuver tactics on the peninsula, General Stonewall Jackson was making an immortal name for himself with his diversionary actions in other areas of Virginia.

The moment the evacuation of Yorktown was known McClellan moved in pursuit, leaving a strong holding force at Yorktown. After a hot fight resulting in heavy casualties on both sides, the Williamsburg line was broken on May 5th, and Johnston was in full retreat back toward Richmond. Only about one third of McClellan's forces participated in the Battle of Williamsburg; a second third remained at Yorktown; and the remainder moved on up to West Point.

With McClellan's build-up at Fort Monroe and subsequent move up the peninsula, further occupation of Norfolk was considered untenable. After the Confederates evacuated on May 10th, the *Virginia* was run aground at Craney Island, set afire, and burned to the water's edge. The *Monitor* thereupon moved up the James River with a squadron of Union ships in support of McClellan's advance. After the battle of Malvern Hill and McClellan's withdrawal from the peninsula, the *Monitor* was ordered to proceed to Beaufort, North Carolina. Leaving Hampton Roads on December 29, 1862, she went down the next night in a gale a few miles south of Cape Hatteras.

No ships in the world's history have a more imperishable place in naval annals than the *Monitor* and the *Virginia*. Although their action in Hampton Roads was inconclusive, the future design of all warships was radically changed and every wooden ship of the world's navies was made obsolete.

Because the destruction of the *Virginia* opened the James River to a reinforced Union fleet, McClellan decided to unite his forces and proceed with his original plan of using the James as his main avenue of approach to Richmond, operating on either bank as occasion proved advisable. The heavy rains continued and before his three columns could join up, he received orders from Washington to establish communication with McDowell below Fredericksburg and make available to the latter both troops and supplies from the Army of the Potomac. "Herein," he later wrote, "lay the failure of the campaign, as it necessitated the division of the army and caused great delay in constructing bridges; while if I had been able to cross to the James, reinforcements would have reached me by water rapidly and safely, the army would have been united and in no danger of having its flank turned, or its line of supply interrupted, and the attack could have been much more rapidly pushed."

The Peninsular Campaign was abortive only because its ultimate objective, the siege and capture of Richmond, was not attained. It was successful to the extent that Norfolk was again returned to Union hands, the Confederates were driven from the peninsula, and the James River opened as a communication route up to City Point, and the York up to West Point. These accomplishments made possible Grant's campaign during the last year of the War, using the James River in his siege of Petersburg and eventual occupation of Richmond, following almost exactly McClellan's original plan.

Thanks to Johnston's evacuation of the Yorktown fortifications the town escaped what damage would have resulted from artillery fire. Later in the War, December 1863, the Courthouse which was being used as a magazine blew up destroying the building and the Swan Tavern across the street.

It is interesting to note that the operations of the Siege of 1862 repeated, almost identically, those of 1781, covering the same ground and using many of the same fortifications, renewed and strengthened. The farm house that had been used as headquarters by Lafayette became the camp of General Andrew Porter; Washington's First Parallel became the most advanced battery position of McClellan's Third Corps, commanded by General Samuel Peter Heintzelman; and the Moore House once again found itself at the right of the besieger's line.

Another curious highlight of the 1862 Siege is that General Fitz-John Porter, who led the division at Heintzelman's left, achieved the significant distinction for the U.S. Army of making the first free flight ever accomplished over an enemy's line. On the morning of April 11, 1862, he had made an ascension in the famous observation balloon, "Intrepid," operated by Professor Thaddeus S. C. Lowe, when the balloon broke loose from its moorings and drifted over the Confederate lines only 1,500 yards away. Fortunately for Porter, it encountered a favorable breeze and was blown back to descend behind the Union lines.

Professor Lowe had experienced a similar adventure himself the year before on April 20, 1861, when his balloon, the "Enterprise," drifted all the way from Cincinnati, Ohio, to the coast of South Carolina, a distance of eight hundred miles in the record time of nine hours.

Devotees of Jules Verne will recognize immediately these flights of Professor Lowe and General Porter as the inspiration for Verne's imaginary balloon adventure in *Mysterious Island,* one of his most famous books.

At the time of his Cincinnati–South Carolina flight, Professor Lowe was not with the Army; in fact, hostilities bringing about the War had begun only a week before with the surrender of Fort Sumter. He later became attached to the Observation Corps of the Federal Army and was at Yorktown in this capacity. His gas generator tanks and balloon apparatus were stored in the vicinity of the Moore House and may be seen in several of the Brady Civil War photographs.

To Professor Lowe, at Yorktown, came Count Zeppelin, attached to the Northern forces as technical observer for the Prussian Army, and the great German pioneer of modern aviation made his first studies of lighter-than-air craft while with Lowe at the Siege of Yorktown in 1862.

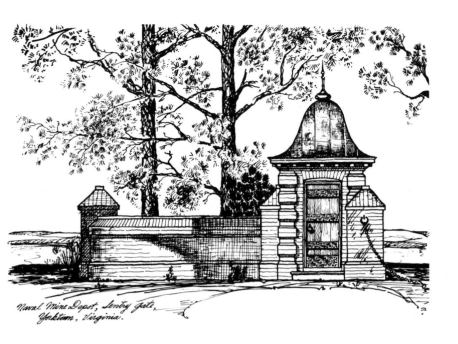

Naval Mine Depot, Sentry Gate, Yorktown, Virginia.

The Naval Weapons Station

D URING World War I, when the United States Navy undertook the stupendous operation of laying the North Sea barrage, it was necessary that there be a plant on the Atlantic seaboard where mines, after being manufactured, could be stored, assembled, loaded, tested, and issued to the naval service in quantities to meet the enormous demands of the War. A place was also needed to train mine personnel in the adjustment and operations of mines.

On August 7, 1918, by Presidential Proclamation, the Navy Mine Depot was established. A tract of land eighteen square miles in area just above Yorktown was selected as the best location on the east coast, being conveniently located with respect to the fuel bases of the Fifth Naval District, the Norfolk Navy Yard, and the Naval Operating Base at Hampton Roads.

Its location on the west side of Chesapeake Bay, ten miles up the York River, particularly lends itself to protection from land and sea. Excellent transportation facilities are available, the railroad forming one boundary of the Depot and the river, navigable by ocean-going vessels of the largest size, forming another. Occupying a long stretch of the heights along the south shore of the York, the area commands a succession of river views unparalled for sheer beauty.

The old Navy Mine Depot was the last Naval station to have "Horse Marines" and the first such Naval base to have a land based airfield with facilities also for lighter-than-air craft.

During World War II the mission and operation of the base were expanded, providing for the testing, storage, and shipping of the latest weapons of modern warfare. The Research and Development Laboratory has since been similarly augmented to handle the more sophisticated nuclear weapons; and on August 7, 1958, the name of the base was changed to the Naval Weapons Station.

The original pier, built in 1919, was supplemented by a second pier in 1940 which was extended and enlarged in 1962.

In spite of the hazardous operations of the station in handling high explosives there has been only one serious accident. In 1943 a load of torpedo warheads exploded killing the loading crew of seven men and completely demolishing the cooling plant in which the ammunition had been stored.

The total acreage of the station is 12,562 acres, making it one of the largest reservations under control of the U.S. Navy, although some eighty per cent of the area is heavily wooded.

Within the limits of the reservation are included the historic acres of Bellfield, Ringfield, and Kiskiack, all of which have been given some notice in the early chapters of this volume, and the sites of old "Cheesecake" Church, Stoney Point, and the Half-way House. The western boundary of the station lies along King's Creek which separates the naval reservation from the land originally patented by John Utie, one of the three first settlers along the York. During World War I Utie's plantation was owned by the DuPont Powder Works and, as the Penniman Munitions Plant, was at that time the scene of tremendous activity. Part of the old Colonial road that winds its way from Williamsburg to Yorktown also passes through the Navy property.

The site now occupied by the Marine Barracks has been known as "Stoney Point" ever since Colonel James Gibbons made it the scene of his residence some time immediately after the Revolutionary War.

As a young lieutenant, Gibbons had been with "Mad" Anthony Wayne and led one of the three advance parties known as the Forlorn

Hopes when the fortress of Stoney Point, New York, was carried by storm. Of his party of twenty men, seventeen were killed or wounded; and for his gallantry on this occasion Gibbons received the soubriquet, "Hero of Stoney Point."

After the surrender at Yorktown, Gibbons, then risen to a Colonel, came to Virginia and made his home near Yorktown at the site above mentioned which he called Stoney Point in memory of his glorious adventure in the North. For many years he was Collector of Customs in Richmond. After his departure from Yorktown the point became part of the eight hundred-acre plantation owned by John Bracken.

Bracken was Professor of Grammar at William and Mary and became President of the college for the two years 1812-1814. He called his home at the Point "Bracken's Castle," and it was quite a commodious establishment. Unfortunately there are no traces of it left today as it was destroyed by fire shortly before the Civil War when it was owned by John Randolph Coupland, great grandson of Benjamin Harrison, signer of the Declaration of Independence. A young Negro slave whom Coupland had brought from his mother's plantation in Alabama, becoming disgruntled over some real or fancied wrong, set fire to an old trunk in the attic and the beautiful old home soon was no more.

Four miles of the road over which Washington and Rochambeau marched their troops from Williamsburg towards the Siege of Yorktown lie within the Station passing the site of the Half-way House, a famous tavern and hostelry of the very early days of the Colony, which is no longer standing. At the Half-way House the French and American troops separated, the former continuing along the direct road to Yorktown, the latter filing off on another road to the right where they were joined by the Virginia Militia under General Thomas Nelson.

General McClellan also marched his army over this same road in his attempted advance up the peninsula during the Civil War. The road leads down through a low, dank ravine formed by one of the arms of Felgate's Creek and bordered by treacherous quicksands. This section has always been known as the Black Swamp and, as every swamp must have its ghostly legend, the Black Swamp of the York is not lacking its tale of mystery and imagination. An old Colonial legend concerns a coach-and-four carrying two beautiful ladies and their escorts back to

169

Yorktown after attending a ball at the Governor's Palace in Williamsburg. While crossing Black Swamp the horses swerved from the road, were engulfed in the quicksands, and horses, coach, ladies, and escorts were all drawn down into the depths of the swamp never to be seen again.

In the murky shadows of dismal swamp nights the local people will tell you that phantom coach swings down the old road; the gay chatter of the ladies may be heard above the clatter of the hooves and the rattle of the harness; and, if you have the fortitude to follow its passage, you will see it drive on down the hill to swerve off the road and disappear again into the morass of Black Swamp.

The Sesquicentennial of 1931

FOLLOWING the victory of 1781 celebrations of any magnitude at Yorktown were few and far between. The first anniversary celebration of the surrender occurred in 1824 when the aging Lafayette visited the site in company with a score or more Revolutionary War officers. Eleven companies of United States troops and twenty companies of Virginia volunteers paraded on the battlefield before an attendance of approximately 10,000 spectators, but the affair was more local or regional in character than one of national interest.

The first truly national celebration of Yorktown Day was the Centennial of October 18-19, 1881. Ten thousand troops paraded before 20,000 visitors. Various units of the State militias from the original thirteen colonies were quartered on the grounds surrounding the Moore House; and army engineers made ready for the assembly of visitors that reached Yorktown by boat from Baltimore, Washington, and New York and overland by a specially built railroad.

The Yorktown Centennial Commission directed the attention of the Federal Government to the long oblivion of the Yorktown site, and Congress was finally moved to appropriate funds for the long authorized victory monument. The cornerstone was laid on October 18th and the monument completed four years later.

The 1881 celebration also brought belated recognition of the historical and geographical relationship between the birthplace of English America at Jamestown and the winning of independence on the battlefield of Yorktown. Another hopeful show of interest was manifest in an attempt by the Yorktown Centennial Commission to raise funds by private contributions for the purchase and preservation of the Moore House. Response, however, was poor and the old building remained in private ownership.

Another result of the 1881 celebration was the formation a few years later of an organization of private individuals with a purpose to "acquire, preserve and restore ancient historic grounds, buildings, monuments and tombs in the Commonwealth of Virginia" to be known as the Association for the Preservation of Virginia Antiquities. In 1907 the association organized the celebration of Jamestown's 300th anniversary, held curiously enough not at Jamestown but in the Norfolk area on a tract of land which in 1917 became the Norfolk Naval Base.

It was not until the approach of the Yorktown Sesquicentennial of 1931 that the Federal Government began a purposeful and large scale program to protect, preserve, and improve the historic sites of both Yorktown and Jamestown.

The United States Yorktown Centennial Commission came into being upon passage of a concurrent resolution of both houses of Congress in May, 1928, augmented in 1930 by the chartering of a private corporation called the Yorktown Sesquicentennial Association. Many interested persons had been thinking in broad terms of arousing governmental interest in the historic unity of Jamestown, Williamsburg, and Yorktown. The planning of the Sesquicentennial celebration provided the catalyst for bringing their ideas into focus.

The Reverend William A. R. Goodwin of Williamsburg, President of the Sesquicentennial Association, advanced the idea that the state of Virginia should acquire Jamestown Island, the Federal Government the Yorktown Battlefield, while a private benefactor (John D. Rockefeller) should undertake the restoration of Williamsburg.

The suggestion that all three areas be included in a proposed Historic Park was advanced simultaneously from such diverse sources as the Virginia Commission on Conservation and Development, the National Park Service, and the Williamsburg Holding Corporation. Enthusiasm for the plan was communicated to Secretary of the Interior, Ray Lyman Wilbur, who won the approval of President Hoover. To give the plan a national character, Representative Louis C. Crampton introduced legislation to create Colonial National Monument that became law on July 3, 1930.

The Yorktown Sesquicentennial celebration of the following year was a four-day affair, October 16 to 19, staged against staggering handicaps. The town at that time had but 300 residents and lacked good highway and railway transportation; facilities and public utilities to accommodate large crowds were non-existent. Federal, state, and private agencies tackled an almost overwhelming task but, with the aid of the military services, were able to feed, seat, and police the attendance that increased daily from 60,000 on October 16th to 150,000 on the anniversary of the 19th, when President Hoover made the principal address.

Preparations for the celebration were undertaken jointly by the National Park Service and the U. S. Army many weeks in advance of the opening date. The battlefield area was cleared; roads, footpaths, latrines, and parking areas established for 24,000 cars; exhibition tents erected and a grandstand built to seat 22,500 spectators. Facilities were provided for the press, telephone, and telegraph companies; concession tents housed restaurants, lunch, and soft drink stands.

Participating naval units anchored in the York River included ships of the French Navy and a large portion of the U. S. Fleet made up of two battleships, fourteen cruisers, nineteen destroyers, and an aircraft carrier and the U. S. S. *Constitution* (now the famous *Old Ironsides*). Hovering over all was the dirigible, *Los Angeles*. All ships were open for public inspection, served by Navy launches from specially constructed docks.

Military units, housed in tent camps, included infantry, cavalry, and field artillery of the U. S. Army, and National Guard battalions from the various eastern states.

Special programs arranged for each of the four days included military displays and drills, pageants, band concerts, dedication of memorial tablets, a Colonial Fair and Harvest Festival, an Indian Village,

Colonial Tilting Tournament, and innumerable speeches. The principal addresses were given by President Herbert Hoover, General John J. Pershing, Marshall Henri Petain of France, and several Cabinet members and Congressmen.

The celebration concluded with a Grand Military Review on the Pageant Field; Army, Navy, Marine, Coast Guard, and National Guard units passing in review before the President of the United States.

In the words of W. M. Robinson, first National Park Superintendent of Colonial National Monument, the celebration ranked "among the major festivals in the world's history."

The Jamestown-Williamsburg-Yorktown Celebration of 1957

T HE celebration of Jamestown's 350th anniversary was an event of far-reaching effect, bringing to the nation's attention the origin and growth of many of our freedoms. Previous celebrations, such as those of 1881, 1907, and 1931, brought many benefits surviving to the present day; but the 1957 observance surpassed them in permanent contributions and vast capital improvements toward better protection and public appreciation of the historic sites that have been called the cradle of the Republic.

Beginning April 1, 1957, and ending November 30, 1957, the celebration was in every respect a great success, attracting almost two million participants and focusing national and international attention on the origin of our free institutions over the long span of Colonial years.

Planning for the 350th anniversary began as early as 1952. World War II and the limitation of Federal funds had kept development plans for Colonial National Historical Park more or less static. With the appointment by the Commonwealth of Virginia of a commission to recommend the kind of celebration to be carried out in

175

1957, reappraisal of the Park master plans in light of the coming anniversary indicated the need for much greater protection and development for public use of both the Jamestown and Yorktown areas. Right-of-way had been acquired for completion of the Colonial Parkway from Williamsburg to Jamestown and the Yorktown terminus, but Federal appropriations for the construction of the roadways were lacking.

Incomplete research and lack of an interpretive program detracted from visitor appreciation. Inadequate parking and sanitary facilities made it apparent that major improvements must be constructed to accommodate the anticipated crowds during the celebration. Visitor information centers were lacking and definite plans were needed for interpreting the areas to the public.

By 1953 National Park Service plans included proposals for completion of the Parkway construction; design and construction of Visitor Information Centers at both Jamestown and Yorktown; construction of a glass-making exhibit at Glasshouse Point and road connections from the point to Jamestown Island, with a tour road through the eastern part of the island. The brick foundations of the original Jamestown houses discovered by an archaeological excavation were to be exposed and the houses themselves depicted by interpretive paintings; the interpretive program was to be carried out by joint agreement with the Association for the Preservation of Virginia Antiquities.

At Yorktown tours of the battlefield area were projected for tourists, and the restoration of Main Street to its eighteenth century appearance proposed.

This early program, planned by the National Park Service staff, was implemented, realized, and completed with Federal funds in time for the opening of the 1957 celebration.

Supplementing the National Park Service planning, in addition to the Virginia State Commission, was a Federal Agency authorized by Congress on August 13, 1953—the Jamestown-Williamsburg-Yorktown Celebration Commission consisting of eleven members. An additional organization, the Virginia 350th Anniversary Corporation, was chartered on December 1, 1954, to handle concessions, enter into contracts, etc. The Travis House in Williamsburg was leased for the various commissions' headquarters; and a program of special observances was planned for the entertainment and instruction of visitors, the prototype of whom was considered to be a hypothetical Mr. Smith, "only mildly history-minded and inclined toward benevolent domination by his wife and two children, aged five and fourteen." As a by-product of the celebration it was proposed that the State Library Board undertake the microfilming of Virginia's colonial records in Great Britain. Plans were also formulated for the recontruction of the colonists' three ships, *Susan Constant, Godspeed,* and *Discovery.*

Three events took place in 1956 preceding the opening of the Festival: first, the laying of the keel of the *Susan Constant* at West Norfolk on March 17, 1956; second, the State Commission joined the Virginia Cruise Corporation in sponsoring a goodwill tour to England, Scotland, Holland, Belgium, and France by a party of 115 Virginians headed by Governor and Mrs. Thomas B. Stanley, to issue personal invitations to Queen Elizabeth II and other dignitaries to visit the 1957 celebration. An official invitation to the Queen was subsequently tendered by President Dwight Eisenhower. Third, on December 20th, all three of the reconstructed ships were christened before an assembly of two thousand. The *Susan Constant* was christened by Mrs. Stanley; the *Godspeed* by Lady Caccia, wife of Sir Harold Caccia, British Ambassador to the United States; and the *Discovery* by Mrs. Lewis W. Douglas, wife of the Chairman of the English-Speaking Union of the United States.

The first event of the Festival was a three-day series of exercises formally opening on March 30th with the dedication of the newly constructed Visitor Centers at both Jamestown and Yorktown, the reconstructed prototype Glasshouse on Glasshouse Point, Jamestown Festival Park, and the new Information Center at Colonial Williamsburg.

The landing of the colonists on American shores was celebrated with a second three-day program beginning on April 26th that included exercises at Cape Henry, Norfolk, and the arrival of the three ships at Jamestown (towed by the Coast Guard). In May the 350th Anniversary was highlighted by Vice President Richard M. Nixon reading President Eisenhower's proclamation establishing May 13th as Jamestown Day.

Throughout the year concurrent events, pageants, military reviews, etc. were held both in the Jamestown Festival Park and in Williamsburg. On June 8th, an International Naval Review took place in Hampton Roads made up of 114 naval vessels including ships from seventeen foreign navies and stretching out almost fourteen miles in saluting the reviewing ships, the United States cruisers *Canberra*, *Boston*, and *Northampton*. Between July 5th and 24th, over 1500 Boy Scouts visited the festival and were billeted by the Army at Fort Eustis.

Events of the Festival reached their culmination with the visit of the British royal party on October 16th and the celebration of the Yorktown Victory on the 18th and 19th. Queen Elizabeth and Prince Philip were greeted on their arrival at Jamestown by a crowd of 25,000. Full military honors were rendered by all branches of the Armed Forces, and after a tour of the Island, the party proceeded to Williamsburg for receptions at both William and Mary College and the Governor's Palace.

The commemoration of the Siege of 1781 and Victory at Yorktown was held there on October 18th, and the anniversary of Lord Cornwallis' surrender on the 19th was the last of the major events with a re-enactment of the Battle of Yorktown and pageantry on the battlefield participated in by Army and National Guard units in Colonial uniform, twenty-two units of the Centennial Legion of Historic Commands and various honor guards, bands, and drum corps from the various eastern states, witnessed by 25,000 spectators.

The celebration brought a substantial increase in visitors to the Jamestown-Williamsburg-Yorktown area from a wide range of income groups, thus achieving the dominant intent of the festival—to draw homage to this free Nation's place of birth from the many who represent American Democracy.

Colonial National
Historical Park: 1970

O N December 30, 1930 President Herbert Hoover, by proclamation, formally established Colonial National Monument that included 2,500 acres at Yorktown and 1,537 acres at Jamestown. The Yorktown area was enlarged to 4,500 acres by Congressional Act in 1931 and with the subsequent inclusion of Colonial Parkway and other acquisitions the Congress, by an act of June 5, 1936, changed the name of the monument to Colonial National Historical Park.

Today the 7,000 acre Park includes Jamestown, Yorktown, Colonial Parkway, and the Cape Henry Memorial. The Park is administered by the National Park Service, U. S. Department of the Interior; Jamestown being jointly administered by the Association for the Preservation of Virginia Antiquities and the National Park Service.

Jamestown, the site of the first permanent English settlement in America, offers the following facilities for visitors:

The Visitor Center contains a theater where the orientation program is presented regularly. Informational services are also available.

The Townsite presents the remains of the Old Church Tower and Statehouse. Excavated foundations of the original houses, taverns, and shops may be seen on a one mile, self-guided walking tour.

179

A five-mile Island Drive winds through 1,500 acres of woodland and marsh, with a series of exhibits interpreting both the land and its early settlers.

A period type Glasshouse has been constructed near the ruins of the original glass furnace of 1608. Here glassblowing demonstrations are conducted daily by costumed workmen.

Yorktown, the scene of the climactic battle of the American Revolution, offers the following attractions:

The Visitor Center offers both a museum and orientation program as well as informational services.

A self-guided tour of the Battlefield area may be made in drives of five, ten, or fifteen miles taking in Redoubts Nos. 9 and 10, the American, French, and British fortifications, Washington's Headquarters, the American and French camp sites, the Moore House where the articles of surrender were drawn up by the emissaries of Washington and Cornwallis, Surrender Field, where the British laid down their arms and the National Cemetery.

A tour of the "Town of York" includes Grace Episcopal Church, a number of restored and reconstructed 18th century houses and buildings, the Cornwallis Cave, and the Yorktown Victory Monument.

Picnic areas, complete with restroom facilities, are provided on the Yorktown Beach behind the Victory Monument; at Ringfield on the Colonial Parkway approximately six miles northwest of Yorktown; and at Great Neck on the Colonial Parkway between Williamsburg and Jamestown.

Yorktown National Cemetery was selected in 1866 as the most suitable cemetery location in the general vicinity of various Civil War battlefields and scenes of action related particularly to the Peninsular Campaign of 1862. The cemetery lies just south of the Confederate line about Yorktown and in the immediate area of the battleground of 1781 where American and French troops won the climactic struggle in the American Revolution.

A total of 2180 persons are interred here; all but fourteen, who were civilians, saw military service in the various campaigns. Some bodies were removed from nearby places, including Williamsburg,

White House Landing, King and Queen Courthouse, Cumberland Landing, West Point, and Warwick Courthouse.

The Colonial Parkway construction, conceived as a scenic highway connection between Yorktown, Williamsburg, and Jamestown was started in 1931, the section between Yorktown and Williamsburg being completed and opened in 1938. In 1940 construction was started on the tunnel under the restored section of Williamsburg but due to the interruption of World War II the tunnel was not completed and opened to traffic until May 10, 1949. The Korean War prevented completion of the Parkway from Williamburg to Jamestown, and it was not until April 1, 1957, that this final section was completed and dedicated. An additional bit of work remained on the Yorktown end, and on April 27, 1957 the entire highway was opened from terminus to terminus.

The completed parkway follows a route unusually rich in scenery, floral beauty, and historical interest, with wide open vistas along the York River, winding stretches over rolling terrain and through tall pine forests across the Tidewater Peninsula, emerging at the James River where it follows the shore line to Glasshouse Point and the approach to Jamestown Island.

Tree and plant life of the area is in many ways unique. Pine, hickory, oak, beech, and tulip trees abound along the route. Yellow jessamine entwines itself on trees to twice a man's height; in early spring the pinkish-white blossoms of trailing arbutus may be seen. Growths of galax, mountain laurel, and camellias, Scotch broom, and the Yorktown onion, or wild leek, are plants peculiar in this part of the world to the Yorktown area.

More than 30 interpretive markers are placed at points of interest along the parkway memorializing sites of historic significance throughout its length.

The Cape Henry Memorial commemorates the approximate site where the Jamestown settlers first came ashore on April 26, 1607. Located within the Fort Story Military Reservation, the memorial consists of a quarter-acre in area, the site being marked by a large Memorial Cross.

181

THE SIGNIFICANCE OF YORKTOWN

By Douglas Southall Freeman

(From the *Yorktown Book*, 1932)

The story of Yorktown is not to be read in the published reports or reconstructed from the weathered redoubts. For the revolution was the most personal of wars. If men believed the uprising a crime against king and conscience, they paid for their conviction in obloquy and in exile. If they held the revolution to be the cause of justice and right, then they gave to it their bodies and their belongings and were likely to lose both in the campaigns that covered the land from Savannah to Saratoga. The victory of Yorktown, to these patriots, was answered prayer, rewarded patience, vindicated faith. The triumph of their arms seemed a miracle. It lay at the basis of the belief, which prevailed in America until the War Between the States, that a special Providence had created a new nation as it had in ancient days preserved a chosen people. This is the spiritual significance of Yorktown and it far outweighs the military and the political importance of that last campaign.

Prior to 1781, successful revolution had been the dream of patriots and defeated rebellion had been their lot. Only the Swiss and the Dutch, the one with their mountains and the other with their dykes, had refuted the maxim that rebellions were raised to be repressed. It was the American's fortune at Yorktown to make the philosophy of revolution dynamic. They faced the odds and they endured disaster. They ran at Monmouth ere they stood at Yorktown. If their cause, which had been brought close to extinction at Valley Forge, could triumph in the end, the apostles of no just cause need ever despair. Wheresoever men read history, Yorktown symbolized the inspiriting truth that resolution works revolution. That was the significance of Yorktown in the world drama of man's political progress, and most of all that was its significance to France. A French king could not fight to win liberty for an alien people and deny it to his own subjects. It was a spark from Yorktown that fired the Bastile.

England, as Sir George Otto Trevelyan was fond of reminding his readers, gained as much from the revolution as America did. She saved one empire at the cost of another. She learned moderation from failure and wisdom from defeat. Never again were the bureaucrats as arrogant as in the days of Lord North. There was Nemesis in this, destruction for the destroyer. To abuse power is to lose it—that lesson Yorktown taught the world.

ARTICLES OF CAPITULATION

The Articles of Capitulation settled between his Excellency General Washington, commander-in-chief of the combined forces of America and France; his Excellency the Count de Rochambeau, lieutenant general of the armies of the King of France, great cross of the royal and military order of St. Louis, commanding the auxiliary troops of his most Christian Majesty in America; and his Excellency the Count de Grasse, lieutenant general of the naval armies of his most Christian Majesty, commander-in-chief of the naval army of France in the Chesapeake on the one part: And the Right Honorable Earl Cornwallis, lieutenant general of his Britannic Majesty's forces, commanding the garrisons of York and Gloucester; and Thomas Symonds, Esquire, commanding his Britannic Majesty's naval forces in York River, in Virginia, on the other part.

ART. I.   The garrisons of York and Gloucester, including the officers and seamen of his Britannic Majesty's ships, as well as other mariners to surrender themselves prisoners of war to the combined forces of America and France. The land troops to remain prisoners to the United States; the navy to the naval army of his most Christian Majesty.

Granted.

ART. II.   The artillery, guns, accoutrements, military chest, and public stores of every denomination, shall be delivered unimpaired, to the heads of departments appointed to receive them.

Granted.

ART. III.   At twelve o'clock this day the two redoubts on the left bank of York to be delivered; the one to a detachment of American infantry; the other to a detachment of French grenadiers.

Granted.

The garrison of York will march out to a place to be appointed in front of the posts, at two o'clock precisely, with shouldered arms, colors cased, and drums beating a British or German march. They are then to ground their arms, and return to their encampments, where they will remain until they are dispatched to the places of their destination. Two works on the Gloucester side will be delivered at one o'clock to a detachment of French and American troops appointed to possess them. The garrison will march out at three o'clock in the afternoon; the cavalry with their swords drawn, trumpets sounding; and the infantry in the manner prescribed for the garrison of York. They are likewise to return to their encampments until they can be finally marched off.

ART. IV.   Officers are to retain their sidearms. Both officers and soldiers to keep their private property of every kind and no part of their baggage or papers to be at any time subject to search or inspection. The baggage and papers of officers and soldiers taken during the siege to be likewise preserved for them.

Granted.

It is understood that any property obviously belonging to the inhabitants of these States, in the possession of the garrison, shall be subject to be reclaimed.

ART. V.   The soldiers to be kept in Virginia, Maryland, or Pennsylvania, and as much by regiments as possible, and supplied with the same rations or provisions as are allowed to soldiers in the service of America. A field officer from each nation, to wit, British, Anspach, and Hessian, and other officers on parole in the proportion of one to fifty men, to be allowed to reside near their respective regiments and to be witnesses of their treatment; and that their officers may receive and deliver clothing and other necessaries for them; for which passports are to be granted when applied for.

Granted.

ART. VI.   The general, staff and other officers, not employed as mentioned in the articles, and who choose it, to be permitted to go on parole to Europe, to New York, or any other American posts at present in possession of the British forces, at their own option and proper vessels to be granted by the Count de Grasse to carry them under flags of truce to New York within ten days from this date, if possible, and they to reside in a district to be agreed upon hereafter until they embark.

The officers of the civil department of the army and navy to be included in this article. Passports to go by land to those to whom vessels cannot be furnished.

Granted.

ART. VII. Officers to be allowed to keep soldiers as servants according to the common practice of the service. Servants, not soldiers, are not to be considered as prisoners and are to be allowed to attend to their masters.

Granted.

ART. VIII. The *Bonetta* sloop of war to be equipped and navigated by its present captain and crew and left entirely at the disposal of Lord Cornwallis from the hour that the capitulation is signed, to receive an aidde-camp to carry dispatches to Sir Henry Clinton; and such soldiers as he may think proper to send to New York, to be permitted to sail without examination, when his dispatches are ready. His Lordship engages on his part that the ship shall be delivered to the order of the Count de Grasse, if she escapes the dangers of the sea; that she shall not carry off any public stores. Any part of the crew that may be deficient on her return, and the soldiers passengers, to be accounted for on her delivery.

ART. IX. The traders are to preserve their property, and to be allowed three months to dispose of or remove them and those traders are not to be considered as prisoners of war.

The traders will be allowed to dispose of their effects, the allied army having the right of preemption. The traders to be considered as prisoners of war upon parole.

ART. X. Natives or inhabitants of different parts of this country, at present in York or Gloucester are not to be punished on account of having joined the British army.

This article can not be assented to, being altogether of civil resort.

ART. XI. Proper hospitals to be furnished for the sick and wounded. They are to be attended by their own surgeons on parole; and they are to be furnished with medicines and stores from the American hospitals.

The hospital stores now in York and Gloucester shall be delivered for the use of the British sick and wounded. Passports will be granted for procuring further supplies from New York as occasion may require; and proper hospitals will be furnished for the reception of the sick and wounded of the two garrisons.

ART. XII. Wagons to be furnished to carry the baggage of the officers attending on the soldiers, and to surgeons when travelling on account of the sick, attending the hospitals at the public expense.

They are to be furnished if possible.

ART. XIII. The shipping and boats in the two harbors, with all their stores, guns, tackling, and apparel, shall be delivered up in their present state to an officer of the navy appointed to take possession of them, previously unloading the private property part of which had been on board for security during the siege.

Granted.

ART. XIV. No article of capitulation to be infringed on pretence of reprisals; and if there be any doubtful expressions in it, they are to be interpreted according to the common meaning and acceptation of the words.

Granted.

Done at York Town in Virginia October 19, 1781.

Cornwallis

Thomas Symonds

Done in the trenches before York Town in Virginia October 19, 1781.

G. Washington

Le Comte de Rochambeau

Le Comte de Barras, en mon nom & celui de Comte de Grasse.

ORIGINAL PURCHASERS OF LOTS – 1691 (AND AFTER)

(* Indicates forfeiture of title due to failure to build within one year)

LOT NO.	NAME OF PURCHASER	LOT NO.	NAME OF PURCHASER
1	Thomas Hill	34	Joshua Broadbent
2	William Buckner	35	York-Hampton Church
3	William Buckner		*(Grace Episcopal Church)*
4	Nicholas Sebull	* 36	William Digges
5	Benjamin Read		*(Site of Somerwell House)*
6	John Sedgwick	37	Thomas Mumford
* 7	Joseph Walker	* 38	John Wills
* 8	Thomas Harwood	39	John Martin
* 9	Robert Leightonhouse	40	Richard Starke
10	Joseph Ring	41	David Condon
	(Given him for services as	42	John Seabourn
	Trustee)		*(Site of Thomas Pate House)*
11	Ralph Walker	* 43	David Taylor
12	Miles Cary		*(Site of Custom House &*
13	Owen Davis		*Ambler House)*
14	Miles Cary	* 44	Cornelius Willson
15	John Trotter	* 45	William Hewitt
16	Lt. Col. Thomas Ballard	* 46	Thomas Chisman
	(Given him for services as	* 47	Daniel Parke
	Trustee)	* 48	William Cary
* 17	Dudley Digges	49	James Bowman
	(Site of Martiau monument)	* 50	John Dunbarr
* 18	Ralph Flowers	* 51	Richard Cheshire
* 19	Thomas Collier	* 52	James Darbisheire
20	Miles Cary		*(Site of Nelson House; York*
21	Robert Ballard		*Hall)*
22	Thomas Chisman	* 53	William Simson
* 23	Francis Cattehill		*(Site of Edmund Smith House)*
24	York County Courthouse Site	* 54	Thomas Sessions
25	Charles Hansford		*(Site of Captain John Ballard*
	(Site of Swan Tavern)		*House)*
* 26	William Thompkins	* 55	James Walker
27	John Dowsing	56	Thomas Sessions
* 28	Symon Stacy		*(Site of Sessions House)*
29	Hector Sessions	57	Thomas Sessions
30	John Rogers	58	Robert Harrison
	(Site of Medical Shop)	59	William Kemp
31	Michaele MacCormack	60	Alexander Young
32	John Northern	61	Alexander Young
33	John Dowsing	62	Robert Harrison
		63	Richard Cheshire

LOT NO.	NAME OF PURCHASER	LOT NO.	NAME OF PURCHASER
* 64	Edward Hill	76	William Cole
65	Edward Moss, Jr.	77	David Stoner
66	William Harwood		*(Site of Dudley Digges House)*
* 67	George Allen	* 78	Ralph Wormley
68	Abraham Archer	* 79	John Myhill
69	William Allen	80	Nathaniel Bacon
* 70	James Sclater		*(Site of Victory Monument which also includes Lot Numbers 81, 82, and 83, following.)*
* 71	George Allen		
72	Major Lawrence Smith *(Given him for services as Surveyor)*	* 81	Joseph Shropshire
		82	Nathaniel Bacon
73	Robert Read	83	Robert Read
74	Robert Read	84	Francis Nicholson
75	Sam Cooper	85	Francis Nicholson

BIBLIOGRAPHY

BOOKS AND ARTICLES:

ARTHUR, MAJOR ROBERT. *The Sieges of Yorktown 1781 and 1862.* Fort Monroe, Virginia: Coast Artillery School Press, 1927.

BASSETT, JOHN SPENCER. *The Relation Between the Virginia Planter and the London Merchant.*

BLOCK, EUGENE B. *Above the Civil War; Thaddeus Lowe, Balloonist.* Berkeley: Howell-North, 1968.

BROUGHTON-MAINWARING, MAJOR ROWLAND. *Historical Record of the Royal Welch Fusiliers.* London: Hatchards, 1889.

BRADFORD, NED. *Battles and Leaders of the Civil War.* New York: Appleton-Century-Crofts, 1956.

BRUCE, PHILIP ALEXANDER. *The Economic History of Virginia in the Seventeenth Century.* New York: Macmillan Co., 1895.

BURKE, JOHN DALY. *History of Virginia from its First Settlement to the Present Day.* Petersburg, Virginia: Dickson & Pescud, 1804.

BYRD, WILLIAM. *The Westover Manuscripts.* Cambridge, Massachusetts: Belknap of Harvard, 1966.

CAMPBELL, CHARLES. *History of the Colony and Ancient Dominion of Virginia.* Philadelphia, Pennsylvania: J.B. Lippincott & Co., 1860.

CHATTERTON, EDWARD KEBLE. *Seed of Liberty.* Indianapolis, Indiana: Bobbs-Merrill, 1929.

CLOS, CAPTAIN JEAN HENRI. *The Glory of Yorktown.* Yorktown, Virginia: Yorktown Historical Society, 1924.

CRIDLIN, WILLIAM BROADDUS. *A History of Colonial Virginia.* Richmond, Virginia: Williams Printing Co., 1923.

DAVIS, BURKE. *The Campaign That Won America.* New York: The Dial Press, 1970.

DODSON, LEONIDAS. *Alexander Spotswood, 1710-1722.* New York: A.M.S. Press, 1969.

EVANS, EMORY. *The Nelsons; a Biographical Study of a Virginia Family in the Eighteenth Century.* Manuscripts, University of Virginia, 1957.

GALLATIN, GASPARD DE. *Journal of the Siege of Yorktown in 1871.* Washington: Government Printing Office, 1931.

GOODWIN, REVEREND EDWARD LEWIS. *The Colonial Church in Virginia.* Milwaukee, Wisconsin: Morehouse Publishing Co., 1927.

187

HENING, WILLIAM WALLER. *The Virginia Statutes at Large.* Richmond, Virginia: Samuel Pleasants, 1809.

HOTTEN, JOHN CAMDEN. *The Original List of Persons of Quality Who Went from Great Britain to the American Plantations, 1600-1700.* New York: G. A. Baker & Co., 1931.

HOWE, HENRY. *Historical Collections of Virginia.* Charleston, South Carolina: Babcock & Co., 1845.

JAMESTOWN-WILLIAMSBURG-YORKTOWN CELEBRATION COMMISSION. *The 350th Anniversary of Jamestown, 1607-1957.* Washington, D.C.: Government Printing Office, 1958.

JESTER, ANNIE LASH AND HIDEN, MARTHA WOODRUFF. *Adventurers of Purse and Person; Virginia 1607-1625.* Richmond: 1956.

JOHNSTON, HENRY PHELPS. *The Yorktown Campaign.* New York: Harper & Bros., 1881.

LAFAYETTE, MARQUIS DE. *Memoirs, Correspondence and Manuscripts.* New York: Saunders & Otley, 1837.

LANCASTER, ROBERT ALEXANDER. *Historical Virginia Homes and Churches.* Philadelphia, Pennsylvania: J.B. Lippincott & Co., 1915.

LARRABEE, HAROLD A. "A Near Thing at Yorktown." *American Heritage:* October 1961.

LOSSING, BENSON J. *Pictorial Field Book of the Revolution.* New York: Harper & Bros., 1851.

LOSSING, BENSON J. *A History of the Civil War.* New York: The War Memorial Association, 1912.

MARTIN, JOSEPH. *Gazeteer of Virginia.* Charlottesville, Virginia: J. Martin, 1835.

MCILWAINE, H. R. *Official Letters of the Governors of the State of Virginia.* Richmond, Virginia: State Library, 1926-1929.

MEADE, BISHOP WILLIAM. *Old Churches, Ministers and Families of Virginia.* Philadelphia, Pennsylvania: J.B. Lippincott & Co., n.d.

MORGAN, WILLIAM J. *The Virginia No Longer Exists.* Lynchburg, Virginia: The Iron Worker, 1960.

MORGAN, WILLIAM J. *The Point Upon Which Everything Turned.* Lynchburg, Virginia: The Iron Worker, 1958.

PHILLIPS, ULRICH BONNELL. *Life and Labor in the Old South.* New York: Grosset & Dunlap, 1929.

RILEY, DR. EDWARD M. *The History of the Founding and Development of Yorktown, Virginia.* Manuscripts, Colonial National Historical Park: Yorktown, Virginia, 1959.

TARLETON, LIEUTENANT COLONEL. *A History of the Campaigns of 1870 and 1871.* Dublin: 1787.

STOUDT, DR. JOHN BAER. *Nicolas Martiau; the Adventurous Huguenot.* Morristown, Pennsylvania: Morristown Press, 1932.

SWEM, E.G. *The Virginia Historical Index.*

TYLER, LYON GARDINER. *Encyclopedia of Virginia Biography.* New York: Lewis Historical Publishing Co., 1915.

VAN LOON, HENRICK. *America.* New York: Boni & Liveright, Inc., 1927.

WILCOX, WILLIAM B. "The British Road to Yorktown." *American Historical Review,* October, 1946.

WILSTACH, PAUL. *Tidewater Virginia.* New York: Cornwall Press, Inc., 1929.

YORKTOWN SESQUICENTENNIAL ASSOCIATION. *The Yorktown Book.* Richmond, Virginia: Whittet & Shepperson, 1932.

OTHER SOURCES:

Calendar of Virginia Papers
Library of Congress, Washington, D.C., Manuscript Division
The Virginia Gazette. Williamsburg, Virginia. 1736-1780
The Virginia Magazine of History and Biography
Virginia State Archives, Richmond, Virginia
William and Mary College Quarterly Historical Magazine
York County Records, 1633-1781, County Clerk's office, Yorktown, Virginia.

Index

Asterisk denotes an entry including several related individuals with the same name.

Ambler, Edward, 81
Ambler, Elizabeth Jacquelin, 81
Ambler House, 82
Ambler, Jacquelin, 81-82
Ambler, John, 81
Ambler, Lieutenant Richard, 33, 77-78, 116, 120
Archer, Abraham, 71
Archer Cottage, 55, 70-72
Archer, Thomas, 71
Archer, Thomas, Jr., 71
Articles of Capitulation, 144, 150, see also Appendix
Association for the Preservation of Virginia Antiquities, 109, 172, 176, 179

Bacon's Rebellion, 22, 26, 38, 41, 44, 90, 111, 116, 118, 145, 153
Ballard, Anne Sayer, 116
Ballard, Catherine, 116
Ballard, Elizabeth, 116
Ballard, Elizabeth Gibbons, 116
Ballard, John, 116
Ballard, Captain John, 112, 114-117
Ballard, Robert, 116
Ballard Street, 42, 44, 98, 119
Ballard, Thomas, 116
Ballard, Colonel Thomas, 116
Ballard, Lieutenant Colonel Thomas, 18, 116
Ballard, William, 116
Beauregard, General Pierre G. T., 157

Bellfield, 18-19, 21-27, 55, 74, 88, 168
Berkeley, Leftenant Edward, 38
Berkeley, Colonel Edmund, 126
Berkeley, Jane, 38
Berkeley, Governor Sir William, 16, 22, 38, 44, 102, 111, 145
Blackbeard the Pirate, 9, 79-81
Blow, Captain George Preston, 110, 114, 117
Brady, Mathew, 82, 104, 122, 148, 166
Bruton Parish Church, 19, 59
Buckner Street, 42-43, 44
Buckner, William, 128
Burton, Ann, 77
Burton, George, 77
Burwell, Elizabeth Carter, 107
Burwell, James, 91
Burwell, Mary Armistead, 91
Byrd, William, 45, 126

Cabot, John, 13
Camp Peary, 30, 31
Carte de la Partie de la Virginie, 136
Carter, Landon, 31
Carter, Robert "King", 31, 77
Carter's Creek, 30
Cary, Archibald, 9, 87
Cary, William, 117
Chevers, The Reverend Mark, 61
Chiskiack, see Kiskiack
Chisman, Elizabeth Read, 111
Chisman, Captain Thomas, 111

189

Clinton, Sir Henry, 132-136, 140
Cole, William, 74
College Creek, 14, 37
Colonial National Historical Park, 7, 45, 56, 149-150, 173-176, 179-180
Colonial National Monument, see Colonial National Historical Park
Committees of Correspondence, 87-88
Cornwallis, Earl Lord, 9, 16, 32, 55-56, 61, 71-72, 108-109, 120, 126, 129, 131-137, 140, 142-143, 151-152, 178
Courthouse, 61-62, 77, 91-92, 98, 103-105, 118-123, 165
Croshaw, Major Joseph, 22, 30
Croshaw, Captain Raleigh, 30
Custom House, 76-83

Daughters of the American Revolution, 82-83, 153, 154
Davis, Jefferson, 157, 163
Declaration of Independence, 109, 169
Delaware, Lord, 21, 30
*Digges, Cole, 24, 46, 74, 86, 98
*Digges, Dudley, 22, 24, 74, 84-88, 99, 115
Digges, Governor Edward, 18, 22-26, 49, 74, 86, 88
Digges, Elizabeth Wormley, 86
Digges Family, 9, 24-25
Digges, Judith, 86
Digges, Lucy, 86
Digges, Martha Armistead, 86
Digges, Mary, 86
Digges, Patsy, 86
Digges, Susanne Cole, 24, 74
*Digges, William, 23, 25, 26, 92
Dundas, Lieutenant Colonel Thomas, 137, 142-143
Dunmore, Lord, 31-32, 87, 101

Felgate, Captain Robert, 17, 21, 29, 39, 145
Felgate, William, 17
Felgate's Creek, 21, 169
Fire of 1814, 55, 61, 71, 74, 82, 91, 117, 121, 122, 127
Fuller, Edward, 115-116
Fuller, Sarah Martiau, 41
Fuller, Stephen, 116
Fuller, Captain William, 41

Gadsby's Tavern, 95
Gallatin, Baron Gaspard de, 82
Gallows Row, 80
Gibbons, Colonel James, 168-169
Gibbons, John, 116
Gibbons, Lawrence, 99, 127
Gibson, Peter, 98, 115
Gibson, Use, 98, 115
Glasshouse Point, 176-177
Gooch, Major William, 49, 59, 83
Grace Episcopal Church, 9, 42, 44, 57-62, 67, 92, 106, 107, 121-122
Grant, U.S., 157, 165

Grasse, Comte de, 16, 44, 82-83, 131, 134-135 143
Graves, Admiral, 135
Griffin, Dr. Corbin, 117, 125-127
Griffin, Dr. John Taylor, 91
Griffin, Mary Berkeley, 126
Griffin, Major Thomas, 91, 114

Half-way House, 168-169
Hampton Parish Church, 59, 115
Hampton Roads, 15, 16, 108, 140, 152, 158,-159, 160-161, 164, 178
Hansford, Thomas, 26, 98
Harvey, Governor Sir John, 22, 37, 39, 42, 144
Haynes, Christopher, 77
Heath, Major-General William, 136
Heintzelman, General Samuel Peter, 165
Henry, Patrick, 9, 87-88, 113
Hoover, President Herbert, 56, 173-174, 179

Indian Field, 30
Indian Uprising of 1622, 22, 38-39, 41, 111
Indian Uprising of 1676, 16, 38

Jacquelin, Edward, 81
Jacquelin-Ambler House, 81
James, David, 113
Jameson, David, 75, 112-113
Jameson, David, Jr., 113
Jameson, Lieutenant Colonel John, 113-114
Jameson, Mildred Smith, 112-113, 146
Jamestown Island, 56, 66, 81, 172, 176
Jefferson, Thomas, 49, 87, 123
Jenings, Edmund, 30-31
Johnston, General Joseph E., 157, 162-164
Jones, The Reverend Scervant, 19-20, 25, 61, 99

King's Creek, 17, 168
Kiskiack Indians, 28-36, 38, 40, 52-53, 118, 145
Kiskiack Settlement, 13, 16, 19, 21, 26, 28-36, 38-40, 55, 59, 67, 144, 168

Lafayette, General, 32, 49, 55, 91, 109-110, 131-134, 140, 171
Laurens, Lieutenant Colonel John, 137, 142-143
Lee, Francis Lightfoot, 30
Lee, Colonel "Light Horse" Harry, 30
Lee, Henry, 29-30, 144-145
Lee House, 29-30, 67, 120
Lee, Richard Henry, 30, 87, 109
Lee, Richard, 30
Lee, General Robert E., 30, 31, 157, 162
Leightonhouse, Elizabeth, 92
Leightonhouse, Robert, 92, 98
Lightfoot, Anne Burwell, 91
Lightfoot, Armistead, 91
Lightfoot, Francis, 90
Lightfoot House, 90-92
*Lightfoot, John, 90, 91

Lightfoot, Mary Armistead Burwell, 91
Lightfoot, Mary Walner, 92
*Lightfoot, Philip, 9, 90, 91-92, 116
Lightfoot, Richard, 90
Lightfoot, William, 91, 92
Lightfoot's Landing, 91
Lincoln, Abraham, 156-158
Lincoln, General Benjamin, 140, 143, 152
Ludlow Family, 9, 113, 145, 148
Ludlow, George, 144-145
Ludlow, Lieutenant Colonel Thomas, 145

McClellan, Major George B., 9, 16, 69, 157-158, 160-165, 169
McDowell, Brigadier General Irwin, 156-157, 165
Magruder, Major General John B., 153, 158-159, 161-164
Main Street, 44, 66, 69, 74, 76, 86, 92, 98, 106, 117, 119, 123, 125, 176
Martiau, Jane, 41
Martiau, Captain Nicolas, 9, 29, 36, 37-43, 49, 144
Martiau, Nicolas, Jr., 41
Meade, Bishop, 59, 147
Medical Shop, 124-127
Merrimac, 16, 159, see also Virginia
Middle Plantation, 31, 40
Monitor, 16, 158-160, 164
Monroe, Fort, 158-159, 160, 164
Moore, Captain Augustine, 147
Moore, Augustine, 113, 146-148
Moore, Bishop, 61
Moore House, 55, 112, 113, 137, 142-150, 154, 165, 171-172
Moore, Lucy Smith, 113; 146-148
Mountfort, Joseph, 92
Mountfort, Captain Thomas, 98, 125

Naval Weapons Station, 16, 20, 25, 30, 56, 167-170
Navy Mine Depot, see Naval Weapons Station
Navy Yard at Norfolk, 156, 158, 167, 172
Nelson, Elizabeth Carter Burwell, 107
Nelson, Francis Tucker, 107
Nelson House, 9, 66, 72, 90, 106, 110, 117
Nelson, Lucy Grymes, 108
Nelson, Margaret Read, 107
Nelson, Mary, 107
Nelson, Sarah, 107
Nelson Street, 44, 66-67, 106, 109, 111, 114, 115, 117
Nelson, Thomas "Scotch Tom", 98-99, 106-108, 116
Nelson, "Secretary" Thomas, 107-109
Nelson, General Thomas, Jr., 42, 49, 62, 71, 83, 88, 91, 99, 106, 107, 108-110, 112, 113-114, 120, 126, 148, 152, 169
Nelson, "President" William, 99, 107-108, 122, 151-152
Newport, Captain, 9, 13
Nicholson, Elizabeth Digges, 88

Nicholson, Royal Governor Francis, 58, 119
Nicholson, Robert, 88
Noailles, Viscount de, 137, 142-143

O'Hara, Brigadier General Charles, 140, 152
Old Point Comfort, 133, 134
Old York Plantation, 144

Page, Elizabeth, 25
Page, Captain Francis, 25
Pamunkey Indians, 21, 29
Pamunkey River, 13, 15, 21
Pate, Elizabeth, 73
Pate, Thomas, 73-75, 98, 113
Pearl Hall, 117
Pendleton, Edmund, 87, 109
Peninsular Campaign of 1862, 16, 156-166, see also Siege of 1862
Percy, Honorable George, 22
Pershing, General John J., 41, 174
Pope, Dr. Matthew, 69, 125
Poplar Neck, 30, 31
Porter, General Fitz-John, 165-166
Porto Bello, 30, 31-32
Potomac River, 15, 43, 61, 79, 156, 158
Powell, Elizabeth Digges, 117
Powell, Dr. Thomas, 117
Powers, Edward, 92
Powers, Elizabeth Somerwell, 92

Queen's Creek, 30, 31, 32, 37

Raleigh Tavern, 87, 95, 99, 100
Randolph, Edmund, 31
Randolph, Peyton, 87, 120
Rappahannock River, 15, 38, 43, 145
Read, Benjamin, 9, 19, 36, 42, 43-45, 73, 144, 145
Read, Elizabeth Martiau, 41-43
Read, Colonel George, 41-43, 111
Read, John, 107, 111
Read, Margaret, 107
Read, Robert, 98
Read Street, 44, 74
Reconstruction, 123, 148-149
Ring, Edmund, 18
Ring, Isack, 18
Ring, Joseph, 18-19, 24
Ringfield, 17-20, 24, 25, 168
Ripon Hall, 30-31
Rochambeau, Count de, 134, 142-143, 149, 152, 169
Rockefeller, John D., Jr., 40, 149, 172
Rolfe, John, 35
Ross, Major Alexander, 137, 142-143

Saint-Simon, Marquis de, 135-137
Scasbrook, Colonel John, 41
Scasbrook, Mary Martiau, 41
Sclater, Mary Nutting, 112
Sclater, Richard, 112
Scott, General Winfield, 156-158
Sessions, Hester, 66

Sessions House, 63-69
Sessions, Thomas, 63-69, 98, 115
Sheild, The Reverend Mr. William, 59, 60, 147
*Sheild, Conway H., 69
Sheild House, 69
Siege of 1781, 32, 54, 55, 61, 69, 72, 88, 91, 92, 105, 106, 109, 113, 120, 126, 127, 128, 131-141, 142, 144, 146, 148, 151-154, 165, 169, 178
Siege of 1862, 55, 69, 82, 150, 165-166
Smith, Agnes Sclater, 112, 146
Smith, Edmund, 111-114, 117, 146
Smith, Captain John, 9, 13-16, 21-22, 28, 33-34, 40, 49, 63
Smith, John, 146
Smith, Colonel Lawrence, 111-112, 146
Smith, Major Lawrence, 9, 18, 44-45, 70, 111-113, 120, 145
Smith, Lawrence, 99, 112
*Smith, Mary 92, 112
*Smith, Mildred, 112, 121, 146
Smith, Mildred Chisman, 111
Smith, Mildred Read, 111
Smith, Robert, 146
Smith Street, 44
Smith, Thomas, 112
Smith's Creek, 43
Somerwell, Elizabeth Leightonhouse, 92
Somerwell House, 72, 89-94
Somerwell, Mungo, 89-94
Spotswood, Governor Alexander, 49, 51, 59, 78-81, 147-148
Spotswood, Anne Katherine, 147
Sumter, Fort, 156, 166
Surrender Field, 152, 154
Swan Tavern, 61, 67, 95-105, 107, 123, 165

Taylor, Captain Daniel, 77, 98
Taylor, Mary, 98
Temple Farm, 113, 144, 145-148, 153
Temple, Peter, 31, 145, 148
Travis, Colonel Edward Champion, 31
Travis House, 176

Treaty of Paris, 92, 141

Utie, Captain John, 29, 39, 118, 168

Vaulx Hall, 30, 31
Vaulx, Robert, 31
Victory Monument, 55, 151-155, 172
Virginia, 158-161, 164
Virginia Gazette, 102, 103, 107, 112, 117

Walker, Joseph, 99, 107
Waller, William, 19, 25
War of 1812, 16, 32, 114
Warner, Augustine, 41
Warner, Mildred Read, 41
Washington, Augustine, 41
Washington, George, 15, 31-32, 38, 41-42, 43, 49, 88, 109, 129, 131-137, 140, 142-143, 152, 165, 169
Washington, Lawrence, 41
Washington, Mary Ball, 41
Washington, Mildred Warner, 41
Wayne, "Mad" Anthony, 132, 134, 168-169
West, Anne, 22
West, Elizabeth, 88
West Family, 9, 26, 29
West, Captain Francis, 22, 144
West, Captain John, 21-22, 39, 144
West, Lieutenant Colonel John, 22, 30, 88
West, Major John R., 88
William and Mary, College of, 31, 52, 63, 88, 178
Williamsburg Gazette, 44, 146
Windmill Point, 128, 130
Wormley, Colonel Christopher, 38
Wormley Creek, 19, 38, 59, 113, 144, 147
Wyld, Thomas, Jr., 82, 91

York Hall Estate, 114
York-Hampton Parish Church, 58-62
Yorktown Battlefield, 172
Yorktown Creek, 39, 128
Yorktown National Cemetery, 151